Keepdate Publishing 2002.   £35

THE
MEDIEVAL
CHURCHES
OF
NORTHUMBERLAND

by

G.W.D. Briggs

Keepdate Publishing

Published by Keepdate Publishing Ltd.
21 Portland Terrace, Jesmond
Newcastle upon Tyne NE2 1QQ

© G.W.D.Briggs
© Photographs by G.W.D.Briggs

First edition published in 2002

ISBN 1 899506 45 4

Designed and typset by
Keepdate Publishing Ltd, Newcastle upon Tyne

An introduction for visitors to

THE MEDIEVAL PARISH CHURCHES

OF

NORTHUMBERLAND

For Edythe

CONTENTS

CONTENTS

CONTENTS

PLATES

The Setting
1 Alwinton. St. Michael. On the fringe of the Cheviots.
2 Stamfordham. St. Mary. A pastoral vale.
3 Corsenside. St. Cuthbert. The open moor.

Anglo Saxon
4 Bywell. St Andrew. Tower from N: Original divided belfry opening.
5 Bolam. St Andrew. W. face of tower.

Norman
6 Old Bewick. Holy Trinity. Nave and chancel with apse.
7 Throckrington. St. Aidan: Vaulted chancel with rebuilt nave.
8 Seaton Delaval. Our Lady. Interior looking E. with twin arches.
9 Norham. St. Cuthbert. Late 12C S. arcade and chancel arch.
10 Warkworth. St. Lawrence. N. nave wall.
11 Heddon. St. Andrew. Chancel interior with vaulted bay.

Late 12C Transitional
12 Alnham. St. Michael. Chancel arch looking E.
13 Newburn. St. Michael. Nave N. arcade with later S. arcade.

13C Early English, Lancet Period
14 Haltwhistle. Holy Cross. From S.E.
15 Ovingham. St. Mary. Long lancets of chancel and S. transept from E.
16 Corbridge. St. Andrew. S. chancel wall.
17 Bamburgh. St. Aidan. The impressively large chancel from S.E.
18 Ovingham. St. Mary. S. arcade with tall and slender round columns.
19 Bywell. St. Peter. The chancel interior, deceptively small with elongated E. lancets.
20 Whalton. St. Mary Magdalene. The unique chancel aisle column with its emphatic dogtooth ornament.
21 Whalton. St. Mary Magdalene. An impression of the 13C interior.
22 Haltwhistle. Holy Cross. Stepped sedilia with their restrained moulding.

PLATES

ACKNOWLEDGEMENTS

Any writer on the churches of Northumberland must be deeply indebted to those authorities who have previously studied the district, notably Sir N. Pevsner, H. L. Honeyman, J. E. Morris and the authors of numerous papers contributed in recent years to Archaeologia Aeliana. Wider aspects of the medieval church are found in books by A. Hamilton Thompson, G. H. Cook, Richard Morris, Colin Platt and Alec Clifton Taylor. These are the sources from which the present writer has derived inspiration, and the background against which he has ventured to offer some original thoughts and comments derived from many years of visiting the buildings described.

The publication of this book has been made possible by generous support from the Sir James Knott Trust; the Barbour Trust; Mrs Margaret Ash; the Bishop of Newcastle; the William Leach Charitable Trust; and the Continuation Charitable Trust.

The author is especially indebted to Bishop Martin for his foreword and most kindly encouragement. To Canon and Mrs. Gofton, late of Whalton, belongs the credit for initiating the book and attracting the funds which enabled it to be completed. The writer owes far more than he can express to their sustained and active interest. Our thanks are also due to Dr. Marshall and his team of Keepdate Publications for their dedicated care in its production. All photographs are by the author.

FOREWORD

I sometimes tell my fellow Bishops that none of them has a lovelier part of England in which to work and minister than I have.

Northumberland offers a landscape of dramatic contrasts – from the heather clad Cheviot Hills to the white sands of Bamburgh, to the isolated splendour of Hadrian's Wall. This is the land of the Northern Saints – the land of Paulinus and Cuthbert and Aidan. It is the land where the Lindisfarne Gospels were written. So it is hardly surprising that a key feature of this beautiful landscape is the medieval parish church.

In this welcome book, Geoffrey Briggs gives us a guide to seventy of them. Here is a gift of love and devotion from the author, a sharing of the pleasure and delight that he has discovered through visiting and exploring these wonderful churches.

Through this book, my hope is that you will be led to enjoy more fully the treasures that are to be found here, to see how these churches have developed over the centuries, to discover the ways in which they have influenced the lives of their people and to catch in them something of the vision of God which inspired their building and still sustains their people and communities today.

These wonderful medieval churches have been hallowed by the continuous prayer and praise of faithful Christian people down the centuries. My prayer is that you too will be led to "Worship the Lord in the beauty of holiness".

Rt. Rev. Martin Wharton
Bishop of Newcastle

PREFACE

Northumberland has many attractions for the visitor ranging from an extensive coastline safeguarded, with other properties, by the National Trust, to the lone walks of the Cheviots, the fertile river valleys spaced by wider moorland, and the major spectacle of the Roman wall with the forts and museums. Amongst these, the churches of the county tend to be overlooked and certainly we shall not find anything to compare in scale with those of such districts as East Anglia. Yet, there is a rewarding area of interest here for a visitor inclined to explore, and it is in the hope of adding to the enjoyment of such, and opening the way to a subject charged with unexpected pleasure, that this small book has been produced. Of the enduring effect that the churches and their surroundings have had upon the writer, the occasional verses will bear witness, hopefully without distracting those whose interest lies in the descriptive text!

INTRODUCTION

Northumberland is to a large extent a county of 13C churches. Out of a total of some sixty-odd about half display major schemes of this period, including fifteen nearly complete chancels. So repeatedly, we meet this austere but refined and dignified style pioneered notably by the Cistercian monasteries of Yorkshire. The narrow pointed lancet windows are everywhere, as are arcades with pointed chamfered arches, their capitals and bases joined to octagonal columns. Interiors tend to be dark except where they are relieved by later windows. Decorative motifs are used sparingly but are worth seeking, for instance at the points where hood mouldings of arcades meet above the capitals. The achievements of the period in developing an art form of spacing and proportion from a restricted vocabulary are widely illustrated and one of the foremost pleasures offered to the interested visitor. The attractive preceding style of plain round arches freed from excessive Norman decoration is also well seen at Longframlington, and at Bolam where the nave arcade has clustered columns. From the late 12C, design developed continuously if unevenly, and we find naves such as Holy Island and Newburn with arcades of different pattern on each side, showing that aisles were added successively as need arose or as funds allowed. This is especially noticeable at times when style was changing quickly, as it was about 1200.

In so many more southerly counties the impression is of 14C and 15C achievements, such as the majestic series of churches stemming from the wool industries of East Anglia. Northumberland was a fairly prosperous and settled area in the 13C, and by its end was well provided with good churches, capable of lasting for a century with only minor maintenance. But when that time came, and updating with extensions was called for, the local scene had changed radically due to the onset of the wars of Scottish succession, church building was inhibited and fabrics began to suffer. It was not entirely that churches were actually destroyed, although that did happen, but that funds were no longer available from impoverished or depopulated parishes for their proper upkeep and extension. Nor did it mean that building activity ceased; on the contrary, the 14C and 15C saw great activity in the modernising of large siege castles and the provision by wealthy landowners of defensible tower houses, often of advanced design, such as Belsay and Chipchase.

But churches must in general have had low priority for funding, with some notable exceptions, and as their condition worsened blocking of arcades and shedding of aisles began so as somehow to keep buildings in use. Such alterations were only remedied in quite recent years at places like Ingram and Newbiggin. The rather strange result is that 13C churches were often preserved, whereas in such districts as East Anglia or the south west, 14C and 15C prosperity induced so much re-planning of parish churches that the 13C style is, comparatively speaking, rare. This inversion is one of the attractions of the scene in Northumberland.

Nevertheless, such 14C churches as the county possesses are of interest and variety, ranging from provincial roughness at Elsdon, to refined decoration suggesting imported skills as at Morpeth, or a happily welcoming and adventurous scheme like Widdrington. The state of the county in the 15C was indeed lamentable, yet it produced the fine town church of Alnwick and the secluded, astonishing hamlet church of Beltingham.

Then we must consider earlier periods, for in the above remarks chronological order has been discarded so as to sketch a general architectural impression. Most churches were already founded by the early 13C, and this means that much Norman and Anglo Saxon building has inevitably been replaced, or survives only in fragmentary form such as the single respond at Whalton or even odd stones re-used in walling as at Alnwick and Bothal. A large Norman church is uncommon in any environment and is usually promoted by special circumstances. Norham, beside the Bishop of Durham's castle on the Tweed is a clear example, Warkworth and Mitford also pointing to wealthy patrons, and we are fortunate too in having small but substantially complete members at such sites as Seaton Delaval and Old Bewick. Of Anglo Saxon naves there are only tantalising fragments such as found at Whittingham and Woodhorn, but a valuable series of towers, four in the Tyne valley, with Bolam and a sadly incomplete Whittingham to the north. Tower building being expensive, slow and even dangerous, these very well built and durable early towers were carefully preserved by medieval masons when other parts of a church were wholly rebuilt. It is also known that considerable remains of these early years lie beneath existing fabrics, and may have influenced some of their less accountable planning. Nor is this the only loss, for the number of chapels serving isolated communities exceeded the number of parish churches, and only a few survive complete, others being slight ruins or merely documented sites. Yet in many ways they comprised the dominant pastoral unit and their loss is to be regretted even though they were rarely of architectural distinction.

We are then concerned with those that allow a visual impression today, remembering that what we see is a pattern of survival and only partly an indication of building activity. The largest tend to cluster along the river valleys, which imparts a strongly E – W grain to the picture. But apart from the sub-pattern of 13C transeptal churches with early towers around Hexham, there are no strongly marked localisations. The most interesting later medieval buildings do tend to group towards the centre of the county between the Wansbeck and Coquet valleys, and the smaller less developed ones in its northern parts, but the general distribution away from the hill districts is wide, and in none of those parts are we far from a site worth visiting.

The descriptions, which follow, do not aim in any way towards completeness, but rather try to capture the essential quality, one might almost say personality, of a church, and to set it in the scheme of building sketched above. This may be especially helpful on a first acquaintance, when a visitor with limited time will not wish to be overwhelmed with information, but rather to sort out what is of primary interest and what they might wish to pursue further. Many of our churches are now provided with useful guide books, often by local historians, and these afford fuller descriptions and open the way to repeated exploration and eventual resort to more specialised literature, for those who may wish to do so.

Technical terms have been kept to a minimum and are often self-explanatory, though one or two, which are frequently used, may seem strange. Thus a piscina is a bowl containing a small drain, and marks the site of an altar; sedilia are low recesses in a chancel wall forming seats for the clergy; a respond, often a half pillar, is the support placed where an arch dies into a wall face; an abacus is the top unit of a capital from which the arch springs. But no one should allow architectural shorthand to hinder enjoyment of a building.

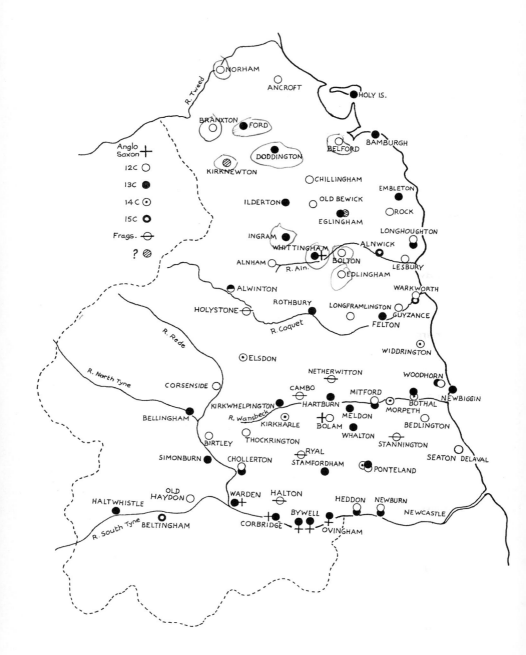

Medieval churches of Northumberland.

ALNHAM. St. Michael.

The lonely church nestles into the Cheviot foothills, in what must have been a vulnerable situation in the years of fierce border raiding from the end of the 13C. This aspect is reinforced by the presence to the west of a fortified vicarage with prominent modern battlements. Then on rising ground facing the church to the south are clearly defined mounds identifying the site of quite a considerable castle.

The foundation of the church is earlier than these buildings, and might possibly have been pre-Conquest, as suggested by the very large quoins at the E. angles of the nave. There is no aisle on the S. side but there is a small plain projecting chapel, which though not in itself archaic could be reproducing the form of an early feature. External masonry is roughly coursed and finished, looking entirely in keeping with the remote environment.

From within, the church reveals a history of several stages, its form having been established in the late 12C when there was an active period of building in the Aln valley. The chancel arch is round, or more properly elliptical, well built in two orders (*plate 12*). The long chancel provides considerably more space than a choir and sanctuary of the earlier 12C would have done, and there is a restored but handsome shafted lancet in the W. gable.

Extensions of the plan came in the 13C when a N. aisle was added to the nave. This was blocked during years of hardship, but the outline of its arches can still be detected on the exterior. Habitation and use continued at least at intervals throughout the later middle ages, as is indicated by the worn but good quality grave covers laid in the chancel floor, and by the fine moulded tomb recess with blank shields in the S. wall. Amongst post-medieval features are the font dated 1664, ornamented with a five pointed star and crescent, a tombstone of the Alder family with curiously mis-spelt and spaced inscriptions, and an unusual modern fireplace at the W. end with a joggle jointed canopy that a medieval mason would surely have approved.

The more recent history of Alnham church was one of increasing decay bringing it to the verge of ruin; as recently as 1947 there were gaping holes in the roof, but it is now well cared for and we must feel grateful for the survival of this small building which stores so much history in stone.

THE MEDIAEVAL CHURCHES OF NORTHUMBERLAND

ALNWICK. St. Michael.

As we approach through the churchyard, the feeling grows that here at last we find a late medieval church that seems to belong to a thriving market town, despite its position close to the troubled border (*plate 34*). No doubt it has benefited, as has the walled town, from proximity to the large and important castle of the Percies, their patronage implied by the crescent and fetterlock badges discoverable in porch and chancel. Originally a modest chapel attached to Lesbury, it had far outgrown the mother church by the 14C. Fragments of an important building of that period remain, but it had been damaged or fallen into disrepair by 1464, when grants became available for a comprehensive rebuilding in the Perpendicular manner. The ground plan is fully developed with wide aisles extending to the full length of the chancel, a type now found only in St. Nicholas' cathedral Newcastle. A stair turret rising above roof level at the SE corner has formerly served a priest's room or vestry above the chancel. The rather squat tower is enhanced by the many-stepped buttresses, which help the eye to make the most of its height. It is placed at the W. end of the S. aisle either because of the steep fall in the ground or from a desire to have a large window in the W. gable to light the end of the long nave. The combined length of nave and chancel seen on entering is most impressive, though perhaps one has the feeling that a wide screen would have blended better with the interior than the retained chancel arch. But masonry skills are everywhere evident, both structurally in the enlarged buttress which takes the thrust of the chancel arch, and decoratively in the sunk panels of the hexagonal N. arcade columns and the carved vine branches with angels holding shields of the chancel capitals (*plate 35*). Clearly the patrons of this work were able to engage advanced skills.

The effigy of a 14C lady lying near the S. chancel wall is finely sculptured, and nearby is an uncommon figure in civilian costume, prompting us to wonder at the evidence of commercial wealth in such a locality and period. Both have handsome carved canopies to their heads, in the manner of the knight's effigy at Warkworth. At the W. end are two statues, one depicting a martyrdom with arrows, the other a standing crowned figure often considered to represent Henry VI.

Those interested in relics of the 14C church may see that the S. arcade differs in style from the N., while the vestry windows have re-used tracery with segmental heads carved from a single stone, but otherwise similar in design to, and perhaps influenced by, some in the Newcastle churches of St. Nicholas and St. John.

At the W. end of the N. aisle is a single-light window with fragments of medieval glass including the pelican feeding her young and a striking face with nimbus, pieces which may have originally belonged to the main windows. The survival of fine craftsmanship in Victorian times is illustrated by the sumptuously carved choir stalls.

ALWINTON. St. Michael.

Is embedded in its hillside quite literally, for it is built against the slope of steeply rising ground (*plate 1*). The level of the chancel is thus higher than that of the nave and this, with the presence of a crypt beneath, results in a flight of ten steps from the nave to the chancel, a rare and striking element of the interior. Though similarly sited, Chillingham has but five steps between levels.

Unfortunately the nave is rebuilding of 1851, possibly including re-used material and to some extent reproducing the appearance of the original with 13C aisles on the N. and S. sides and perhaps a S. transept with foundations underlying the present ones. A fragmentary survival from the N. aisle is a small piscina in the angle of the E. respond as found also at Hartburn, and indicating the former presence of an altar at the E. end of the aisle.

The W. half of the chancel belongs to the 12C and retains an original slit window, but later it was extended towards the E. in a rather similar way to the chancel of Bolam. Later insertions are a two-light window with monolithic 14C tracery in the S. wall opposite to the altar, and two low windows at the W. end. Interesting post medieval memorials are mounted on the wall close to the S. door.

The position of the church is one to be enjoyed, with its open view of hills across the narrowing valley of the Coquet, and the important castle of the Umfravilles less than a mile to the southeast. It is a little strange to find what is in effect a sizeable 13C village church here, though choice of site may date to an earlier time than the existing masonry.

ANCROFT. St. Anne.

Two features of Ancroft church immediately impress themselves. One is the heavy square tower, the other a truly superb Norman S. door, once richly carved but now badly weathered. It makes an interesting comparison with the S. door at Longframlington, built at a later date when Norman ornament had been superseded by a plainer style. Both, like the N. door at Brinkburn priory, project forward from the wall face. A slab with dogtooth edge is now positioned on the threshold.

Closer observation reveals the remains of a small aisless Norman nave with a corbel course like that of Rock, beginning over the door and extending to the W. wall of the tower. This nave remained unaltered until with the later Middle Ages came the era of constant raiding, and Ancroft is very close to the border. Then the tower was built over the western part of the nave with a vaulted basement in the manner of the numerous tower houses, and the S. door was blocked by the SE angle of the tower, which accommodates the spiral stair serving the upper floors. Unmistakable provision for defence can be found in towers such as Bedale in N. Yorks. and Great Salkeld in Cumbria, and is readily implied in churches such as Ancroft where a basement vault has been added.

The Victorian rebuilding of nave and chancel is well worth regarding. It might be described as respectfully imitative of a 12C style, is unusually warm and pleasing and contains admirable craftsmanship and interesting stained glass such as the figure of St. John writing the final words of Revelation.

BAMBURGH. St. Aidan.

One of the largest and finest of Northumbrian churches, it enjoys the splendid backdrop of the castle from its position at the West End of the village. It is clearly transeptal in form with a rather modest W. tower, but its aspect is dominated by the magnificent 13C chancel (*plate 17*). The lancet windows, not so tall as those of the Tyne valley, are placed in pairs between shallow buttresses connected above by a parapet resting on corbels resembling those of the tower of Hartburn. The priest's door is a conspicuous element by reason of its projecting gable, seemingly of recent masonry but likely to reproduce an original design. The fall of the land towards the east discloses a crypt, which supports the eastern part of the chancel.

The nave gives a feeling of even greater size within than when viewed from outside and the indications are that it was laid out before enlargement of the chancel. The primitive 12C impost from which the chancel arch springs is continued into the N. transept, providing evidence for an early chapel on that site. Widening of this chapel is one possible explanation for the short arch at the E. end of the N. arcade, or it may show a reluctance to disturb the angle of the transept, in either instance pointing to a change of plan after the arcade was begun. The building of two long nave arcades of similar design and close date would imply a relatively wealthy parish promoting work comparable with Ovingham on Tyne at a similar period. The columns are uniformly round but now quite slender, showing the progress of building techniques. The capitals are plainly moulded except for one in the N. arcade, which is decorated with formalised foliage. Westward extensions of the aisles to engage the tower are an uncommon development in Northumberland.

The interior of the chancel is finished in a richness appropriate to its size, with hooded lancets joined by wall arcading and there are low windows at its W. end on both sides. It is all the more remarkable that an inadequate chancel arch should have been allowed to remain; whether this was due to disagreement as to who was responsible for rebuilding or a simple desire to emphasise the apartness of the great chancel, is a matter for speculation. Some attempt to improve communication from the nave was later made by providing a large square opening with tracery so that priestly functions could be better seen and heard. A 14C knight's effigy lies beneath an arch in the S. wall.

In returning to the nave, we cannot help being struck by the great width of the S. aisle, which almost absorbs the S. transept. The need for this when a large nave was available is not immediately apparent, although an element of status may be involved as in the similarly wide aisle of Warkworth. One aspect, which remains open to investigation, is the precise influence of the priory of Nostell which maintained a cell nearby and might have had concessions in using the church, as has been documented for the Carmelite Friars of Blakeney in Norfolk.

Access to the crypt is now from outside, and it is a roomy compartment with an elegant pointed ribbed vault in two bays of quadripartite form with an additional E – W rib terminating at the crown. It is quite well lighted and may have served for display of relics as much as for burials.

BEDLINGTON. St. Cuthbert.

Has been extensively rebuilt and altered more than once since the 18C, so that its medieval form is difficult to recover, but it retains an interesting, possibly reconstructed, 12C chancel arch. This has roll mouldings and an order of chevron ornament and is supported by plain concave capitals on short columns, which are continued downward by elongated square bases. If this is an original feature, it anticipates the later and much more elegant design at Longframlington. Evidence of continuing medieval use is to be seen in the niche to the S. of the arch and the interesting group of grave covers inside the W. wall. Little else remains to remind us of a once fine late 12C church.

BELFORD. St. Mary

The chapel of Belford looks, and externally is, almost wholly modern, but it does retain a fine chancel arch from the 12C with scalloped capitals and an order of chevron carved stones. These are only to be found on the E. face and so seen from within the chancel, which leaves the feeling that the arch may have been reset, and for some good reason reversed in the process. There was formerly a S. door of similar design, now unhappily lost. These fragments show that the early chapels of north Northumberland embodied good architectural design, and served their small communities well until either partly or wholly rebuilt like Belford and Rennington, or allowed to lapse into ruin like West Lilburn and Tuggall.

A prized possession of St. Mary's is the Royal arms of George III carved in relief, and at present seen as we enter the S. porch.

BELLINGHAM. St. Cuthbert.

The aspect of Bellingham church is determined by work of two widely separated periods. The form of a late 12C to early 13C building with a S. transept is recoverable and revealed externally by the obtuse pointed and widely separated lancet windows of the E. chancel gable. Within, there is a tall pointed chancel arch rising from rather low responds as at Whalton, and the E. lancets are seen to have acutely pointed and shouldered rere arches. Almost buried in the corners of the nave are capitals belonging to former N. and S. aisle arcades. In the transept a bracket respond with slender shafts and nail head ornament recalls one similarly placed at Ovingham and shows that a W. transept aisle existed.

The very striking appearance of the interior is due to vaulted roofs of about 1600 with close spaced segmental ribs supporting heavy stone slabs. To stabilise the vault, the nave walls were thickened to over four feet, a seeming throw back to early methods of construction. In the event this was not sufficient to sustain the thrust and additional buttresses were added. The pointed tunnel vaults of such Scottish churches as Ladykirk and Dunglass show more accomplishment, but share the object of fireproofing as well as supporting the roof slabs. Similar thinking had previously led to the vaults of chancel and chapel at Kirknewton, and of towers such as Hartburn, Kirkwhelpington and Newbiggin.

BELTINGHAM. St. Cuthbert.

The church overlooks the green space at the bend of the lane passing through the delightful hamlet. It occupies a spur descending steeply on the east to the little stream, the slope when seen thick with snowdrops making an idyllic setting for the great E. window.

Beltingham church is in fact an admirable, if restrained, design of the 15C Perpendicular phase, the only one in the county other than Alnwick to show it in such completeness (*plate 36*). There may have been an earlier building, extending further west, and some of it may be incorporated in the N. nave wall, but the fabric is otherwise homogeneous and of pleasing aspect. This indeed is no provincial attempt. The five windows of three lights with cusped heads are set so close that there is only room for the narrowest of buttresses between them, and this façade will bear comparison with the Lady chapel of Long Melford in Suffolk, which has essentially the same characteristics. Later repairs are perhaps indicated by the date 1691 on the priest's door.

As one would expect, the interior is light, despite the lack of windows in the N. wall, and its impression is dominated by the five-light E. window with well-conceived panel tracery. Division into nave and chancel would have been achieved by a screen.

There are unusual features too. A slit opening with an iron grill on the N. side commands the altar, and would so enable a watch to be kept from a priest's room. Some, however, would prefer to think in terms of an anchorage, though evidence is as yet lacking.

More mysterious are the carved stones inside the surrounds of the S. windows. One's expectation would be to find some connection between these and a wealthy patron, but it is difficult to derive any such logic from these symbols. There are odd carvings on the chancel roof at Lesbury, but those are of doubtful origin.

A pleasing modern feature is glass depicting scenes from the life of St. Cuthbert, patron saint of the church. Here L. C. Evetts has rendered designs, which blend very happily with 15C art, yet without being imitative.

BIRTLEY. St. Giles.

Is to be rated as a tantalising building, for though extensively rebuilt it holds within hints of great antiquity. This is found in the chancel arch, narrow, round and of crude construction. Each face of the arch comprises a single ring of stones, and between them a core of rubble is exposed. It rests on plain imposts, supported by square jambs. There is no architectural detail, so an estimate of the date is unsafe, though we may suspect the 11C as being possible. There are no through stones in an Anglo Saxon manner, but the arch construction is found also at Corsenside and Longhoughton, which seems sufficient to define an established local method.

The other notable possession of the church is the small inscribed stone of Hartlepool type now built into the N. chancel wall. This provides a pre-Conquest link for the site, though nothing of its time may now exist above ground.

BOLAM. St. Andrew.

It stands apart from the world without even a hamlet, in a setting of enviable peace, and perhaps it is hard to believe that there was once a community able to support a pre-Conquest church large by the standards of its day. Yet there before us is the tower (*plate 5*), unbuttressed, pleasantly weathered, with its familiar twin belfry openings divided by a turned shaft which here is capped unusually by a double corbel of the full thickness of the wall. This is found at Jarrow, but most interestingly in the famous church of Sompting in Sussex. A link of some kind is implied, but whatever its nature the message is that Northumberland of the 11C was in the forefront of architectural practice. Closer study will disclose other points of interest such as the course of slanting herringbone masonry just below the parapet and internally the rere arches of windows, which have been widened in the 18C. Here too, as at Whittingham, may be seen the SW angle of the nave, with the aisle W. wall built against it.

Inside, it is the wide S. aisle which immediately attracts attention, but it is well to notice first the nave and remark its narrowness compared with its length. The church standing at the time of the Conquest was undoubtedly a complex structure of which remains are now below ground but whose form has had an influence on later rebuildings, and is probably reflected in the shape of the nave. The visual impression of Bolam however belongs to later periods.

Builders in the Norman style modified the E. end, bequeathing us their fine chancel arch. This was formerly enriched with small grotesque heads, sadly hacked away in the 1870s leaving only the scars. Still, on the E. side of the N. capital two unpleasant examples remain. A S. aisle was added to the nave towards the end of the 12C and its arcade presents a unique aspect amongst the county churches. The well built arches are round without ornament, while the columns are made up of a cluster of four which lend a sense of lightness and delightful contrast of light and shade by being keeled, that is brought to a shallow point. As Pevsner and others have indicated, work of this standard surely originated with the builders of greater churches such as Newminster or Hexham Abbeys.

On moving through the chancel arch we find two short columns and above them some stones with shallow incised saltire crosses. These are likely to be remains of the sanctuary arch, removed when the chancel was enlarged in the second half of the 13C. A set of sedilia was provided and an E. triplet of lancets set close, though separate externally and grouped under one arch internally. The nearby window on the S. shows the next stage, with both lights grouped under a through arch and space created between their heads to form the simplest tracery.

The Bolam chancel is small in area though appearing lengthy because it is narrow, perhaps restricted as at Bywell St. Peter, by earlier chapels flanking its western part. There is now a chapel formed by the nave aisle overlapping its S. side and marked off by an arch carried on brackets, the only structural arch in the church which is pointed. Here are medieval grave covers in the floor, one with a branched stem, the other with the chalice of a priest. Here also has come to rest the broken effigy of a 14C knight, believed to be that of Robert Raymes of Aydon and Shortflatt who died 1324. The entire aisle may have been widened at this time and if so, the attractive S. door with its double row of dogtooth has been moved; there is certainly a misfit in the arch stones consistent with re-erection.

Bolam is a church, which conveys a strong feeling of serenity and repose. Many will find it a place, which seems to bring them close to another level of reality.

BOLTON

The charmingly situated chapel of ease to Edlingham presents only an enigmatic chancel arch remaining from early time. Plastered and whitewashed, it seems to be of primitive construction; a single square edged order resting upon heavy double chamfered imposts similar to those at Edlingham. Current literature sees this as the one early component of the building, but there appears to be original masonry, possibly re-used in the S. chancel wall. The surroundings prompt one to linger, and enjoy also the whimsical Victorian triple arch to the north chapel.

BOTHAL. St. Andrew.

Three routes fall into the hollow where the hamlet of Bothal lies, two of them down steep gradients. Where the road bends sharply, a clear space is overlooked by the bell turret of St. Andrew's. From the churchyard path we see the S. aisle before us, its late medieval two-light tracery windows offering one of the less usual aspects of Northumbrian churches and reminding us that such late building as we have tends to cluster in and near the Wansbeck valley. It is interesting to compare the tracery with the very similar S. aisle windows at Widdrington, six miles to the north, and to notice how the Bothal design is more stiff, beginning to show the rectangular basis of the incoming Perpendicular thinking. This will be found also in the 3- light E. window of the aisle, which yet has hood stops of ballflowers, a very rare architectural plant in this part of the country. The chancel belongs to the 13C lancet series though heavily, and as regards the priest's door, rather aggressively restored.

The N. aisle has similar windows to the S. and so the nave has a pleasantly light ambience. This is an instance where the nave arcades are of notably dissimilar design. The N. arcade appears 13C of four bays possibly later than the colonnette bracket responds, which have some delicate foliage carving. The chamfer stops above the capitals are also worth noticing, for they are carved in the form of leaves, a treatment found also at Whalton and so distinctive as to imply some kind of link. The S. arcade, a later addition of the

14C has three wider arches and no stylish columns, but rather pieces of wall supporting them, as seen for example in an extreme form at Haddiscoe in Norfolk. The arches die into these pieces without capitals, in the way found at Ponteland and the Newcastle churches of St. Nicholas and St. John, but the treatment at Bothal is particularly uncompromising. Two delightful features of the nave now draw our attention. Firstly, the considerable display of medieval glass in the tracery of the aisle windows, amongst the most attractive in a county where such remains are scarce. Between many canopies will be found a shield, Holgrave impaling Bertram, the passion implements, and the Yorkist rayed rose. The E. window of the N. aisle has considerable remains of an Annunciation with 'Ecce ancilla Domine' on a scroll beside Mary. Secondly, the fine alabaster tomb of Ralph Ogle d.1512 and his wife, with weepers round the side (*plate 39*), the county's only example other than the great Grey tomb at Chillingham.

The chancel interior contains a good set of sedilia with piscina, yet we cannot help being struck by the darkness of the lancet building as compared with the lightness of the nave. To see them side by side is to recognise the aim of later medieval periods, striving for more window area to exhibit glass, and to appreciate the limitations of earlier buildings for all their dignity of proportion and fine mason craft. The final surprise is to find original roofs to the nave and aisles, with shields on the nave arch braces held by angels with wings gracefully curved to shape (*plate 40*), all made easier to see by the modest clerestory windows which may be an addition of the same time.

BRANXTON. St. Paul.

The small church lies below the field of the memorable battle of Flodden, and has been rebuilt in the 19C, the only original part remaining being the interesting small chancel arch. The jambs are manifestly Norman of heavy construction with scalloped capitals, but the plain slightly pointed chancel arch with chamfer stops appears to embody later design and is likely to be a 13C replacement.

BYWELL. St. Andrew.

This small church shares an idyllic situation with St. Peter's and has possibly the best Anglo-Saxon tower in the county (*plate 4*). Almost untouched, it has beautifully weathered stones in warm shades of red. Although superficially uniform in appearance, recent authorities have discerned a change of the masonry in the upper stages, which might denote a discontinuity in the building process. There are the characteristic features of large corner stones, belfry windows with mid-wall shaft and the hood found also at Ovingham and at Billingham in County Durham, as well as a rather puzzling door opening below the S. belfry. Whether the porthole openings near the parapet are only decorative or are intended to improve the belfry acoustic is something of an open question.

The remainder of the church has an aisleless cruciform plan of the 13C as found on a larger scale at Warden, but it has been very much rebuilt apart from the lowest wall courses. Within there is a touch of nailhead ornament on the brackets of the S. transept arch and a small 'squint' allowing a view from the transept into the chancel.

A great possession of St. Andrew's is its series of fine medieval grave covers, over twenty of them and some of large size with symbols appropriate to the deceased. This collection was formerly built into the external N. walls and has now happily been extracted for display within the church and so preserved for the foreseeable future.

BYWELL. St. Peter.

Here indeed is a church of many aspects, which has its roots in a minster of pre-Conquest years. It has now been shown that a considerable part of the N. nave wall belongs to these early years, notably the prominent set of high round headed windows. Further, at the point where nave and chancel meet on the N. side can be seen a blocked opening with massive long-and-short jambs and the outline of a gabled roof, marking the position of a chapel, or porticus. Not all this archaic work is necessarily of one date, but its sheer extent makes a strong impression on our sense of antiquity.

Within, we find there is a 13C aisle on the S. side with an arcade of tall slender round columns, looking so similar to the ones at Ovingham that they are possibly by the same master mason. A crowned head terminates one of the arch hoods and there is a mass dial low in the external wall.

The dignified chancel (*plate 19*) belongs to the 13C with a particularly elongated E. triplet having externally an angular hood nearly identical to that used at Haltwhistle. The visual effect of this chancel is extremely interesting for it is amongst the smallest of its kind, yet appears quite large. The reason for this is its narrowness, perhaps because there was an early chapel on the S. as well as the N. and enlargement took the form of increasing its length. The tall 19C chancel arch by Ferrey blends well and looks as if it derived from that of Corbridge.

The squat tower, built on foundations of the W. bay of an early nave, has few openings and is very functional in appearance. Lastly there is the N. nave chapel, well lit with square headed windows having 14C tracery of ogee curved members. It is separated from the nave by two modern arches and houses a worn incised grave slab with faint outlines of a figure in armour dated to mid 15C. No convincing explanation of what seem to be arch springers in the outside wall has yet been devised; they might be related to lost buildings on the N. side, or perhaps the intention was to add an extra aisle as at Ottery St. Mary.

CAMBO.
Holy Trinity.

Has a splendid Victorian tower which, like the similar tower of Stannington, is particularly well sited to form a landmark over a wide area, and would hardly seem misplaced in a wealthy medieval environment such as Northumberland was not to know. But though completely rebuilt, the chapel preserves in the tower basement and vestry, a reminder of its predecessor in a group of fine grave covers, which are well worth turning aside to see (*plate 24*). Most have floriated crosses, one has a stem with branches closely resembling a slab in the S. aisle chapel at Bolam, another an unexplained row of five roundels.

CHILLINGHAM. St. Peter.

To find the church one leaves the Alnwick to Wooler road at the end of the park wall, and passes through the pleasing hamlet with its manor house and former rectory, until a space of green sward overhung by trees appears with the bell turret of the little church above. The steep path encourages a leisurely approach, with time to adjust to enjoyable seclusion. The appearance of the plain building derives mainly from the 12C, though there have been alterations and repairs. There is no aisle, but a small chapel projects from the S. wall with windows having bar tracery. These are evidently additions, for the pointed head of a blocked lancet is also visible, and a round headed slit of even older aspect. The round arched doorway probably came at the end of the middle ages. A circuit of the church will show primitive masonry in much of the walls; especially some huge stones built into the N. nave. So we enter with expectation by a simple 12C door, almost identical with Edlingham, to find surprises within.

First of these is the raised level of the chancel, approached by a flight of five steps from the nave, due partly to the eastward rise of the ground and augmented by the presence of a crypt below the floor, recalling Alwinton on a smaller scale. The plain interior forms an attractive foil to the set of box pews with their numbered doors. The second and greater surprise comes when we mount the steps and see revealed on our right the magnificent table tomb of Sir Ralph Grey d.1443 and his wife, which almost fills the small chapel (*plate 38*). The well preserved alabaster effigies retain traces of colour, while the sides are crowded with figures of saints, amongst which St. Peter (key) and St. Catherine (wheel) are readily identified. Although the effigies are alabaster, the beautifully detailed figures of the sides are actually carved in sandstone in imitation of alabaster work. The source and attribution of this fine piece have still to be determined. Small wonder that this tomb is the essential impression of Chillingham which most visitors will carry away. Yet there is another feature which will not escape notice, the clear glass of the E. window with its vision of lush green foliage instead of coloured figures. This bold approach is sure to have its admirers, though some may prefer the more restrained treatment of the E. window at Meldon.

CHOLLERTON. St. Giles.

Looks at first sight to offer only post medieval building, 18C and 19C. At the gate we notice a stone built shed said to provide stabling for 18C members of the congregation attending services. Tower and chancel are dated to 1769, Gothic detail being added later. All of which leaves one quite unprepared for the remains of a medieval nave, for though the four bay arcades alone survive, these afford valuable testimony and interest. They are of dissimilar date, indicating progressive enlargement of the building, and that on the S. side has capitals assignable to the late 12C, of concave bell shape with square abaci, similar to those found at Lesbury, Widdrington and elsewhere. Remarkably, the columns themselves are in one piece and are generally assumed to be Roman re-used as at Lanchester, Co. Durham and Ickleton, Cambridgeshire. The nearest source would be Chesters and transport by river is probably feasible. The N. aisle was added after a lapse of time in which design had changed, perhaps late in the 13C, and we find octagonal columns with matching capitals. The intriguing point here is that the arches themselves, pointed and double chamfered, are of similar design on each side. So, which is the copy? Both Widdrington and Alnwick pose a similar problem.

A large grave cover in the chancel floor has two crosses with shields and Chollerton also has Jacobean woodwork that should be noticed. It includes a cover for the medieval font, choir stalls and altar back suggestive of re-used domestic fittings, with a miniature Father Smith organ in the N. aisle. All these add a welcome enhancement to an otherwise rather subdued interior.

CORBRIDGE. St. Andrew.

Has developed into a large cross-shaped 13C church, but had its origin in an Anglo-Saxon building of which the tower and part of the N. nave wall have survived. The tower possesses many archaeological complexities but essentially comprises a W. porch later heightened to form a belfry. Traces of a blocked entrance are to be seen in its W. face, while the arch to the nave, of massive build, so much resembles Roman construction that it is often held to have been re-used from a site such as Corstopitum. Later Norman adaptation of the church is marked by the retained S. door, arched in two orders of chevron stones.

Within, we are confronted with a forest of arches as at Ovingham, and an impression of the darkness inseparable from the lancet phase of design. The N. Transept has a W. aisle, and there is an arcade separating the chancel from chapels on the N. side. The plan is then very fully developed for the period, and there are differences of detail in moulding of arches and capitals. These may embody information showing evolution of the church over an extended interval, though to trace this would be an intricate task. Second thoughts have evidently had their place concerning the chancel arch, which is unusually high and makes an awkward joint with the jambs, suggesting that the lower part has been widened.

The chancel S. exterior is one of the most handsome of the series, with a trefoiled priest's door and deep buttresses with small gables (*plate 16*). Although amongst the largest of the 13C, the extension to a N. aisle implies that there was considerable pressure for space. This may be traceable to the small size of the original nave, which is in fact shorter and narrower than the chancel. It is emphasised by the building of transepts and the partial widening of the S. aisle, which stops short of the S. door and suggests an incomplete scheme of the kind fully carried out at Felton.

Although at first sight a somewhat bare interior a closer scrutiny reveals interesting fragments such as the grave cover in the tomb recess of the N. transept and the crude but compelling two headed corbel in the S. aisle. The vicar's tower house standing in the churchyard is eloquent testimony to the hazards of life even in the Tyne valley, in the years which followed completion of the church.

CORSENSIDE. St. Cuthbert.

The lonely church of Corsenside seems not so much to grow out of the wild moorland scenery as to be part of it, and it is seen to perfection against a backdrop of grey wind-driven cloud with intermittent flashes of sun (*plate 3*). One might well wonder, whence came the congregation, yet against the S. wall are headstones and cartouches of notable families of the 17C and 18C, some of them attaining a high level of provincial art. It is difficult to attach a date to a building like this from the very plainness and lack of detail, which renders it of such endearing vernacular aspect. The rugged interior has evidence of antiquity in the plain round chancel arch, its core exposed to view as at Longhoughton and Birtley (N. Tyne) for which at present an 11C date would be as appropriate as any. At the W. end, amongst fragments of grave markers is a dainty figure under an ogee-arched canopy, similar to one found at Haydon Bridge. The windows irresistibly attract attention; perhaps describable as Georgian, the glass has coloured borders more reminiscent of an Edwardian bathroom. So strange a memorial of their time deserves most careful preservation, and seems not at all out of keeping with either the church or the distant scene viewed through the rippled plain glass.

DODDINGTON.
St. Mary and Michael.

Is at first not easy to find in its secluded place behind the hamlet, its isolation emphasised by the small watch house provided to foil the operation of the body snatchers of the early 19C medical schools. And the church itself is decidedly unusual, for in recent times it has 'turned round' so that what we may at first take for the chancel is actually an original western compartment.

We are evidently looking back to a foundation of early 12C at the latest, the revealing detail being the S. respond of the W. arch, a heavy and primitive impost. For the rest, we are in the 13C, shown by original or partly original lancets and a N. aisle arcade which is in the plain local 13C manner with capitals rather coarsely moulded. This aisle stopped when it reached the early W. arch, which was partially rebuilt to match; the nave then continued as an aisleless W. extension, and so it remains today. The small rebuilt choir serves as a baptistery and contains a font with a section of Norman arcading, recalling the discarded one at Eglingham.

Doddington is unique among surviving county churches in its plan and it leaves us with a feeling of holding much that is as yet unexplained.

EDLINGHAM.
St. John the Baptist.

Just as in East Anglia churches built in crisp flint with round towers are inseparable from the scene, so in remote Northumberland are churches of rough grey sandstone which blend with moorland winds and skies. Edlingham, with its plain exterior and modest windows, is a fine instance of the type; it comes almost as a surprise to see a well moulded base course to the rugged tower with its slit windows.

The simple S. door has 12C cushion capitals and some billet ornament on its arch, though one may feel uncertain as to whether the barrel vault of the porch is contemporary. Internally the W. gable with its narrow door and megalithic masonry is likely to be of pre-Conquest build, the tower being a later addition. The nave core and the primitive chancel arch speak to an early Norman reconstruction, followed by the later addition of a N. aisle, which is separated from the nave by an extremely interesting arcade. This is well built with slender columns and round arches of two orders, the capitals being concave and unusually decorated with strips of nail head ornament, also found on the bases. But the size of the capitals is ill suited to the arches, and their design has little relation to that of the bases. There is an awareness of developing architectural practice, but as yet insufficient mastery of it to produce a co-ordinated design, as would be consistent with a late 12C date.

The small church proved quite adequate for local needs and there were no further extensions of the plan. It is significant of conditions in the 14C that the eminent and wealthy owners of the adjoining hall, Sir John Felton and his son, fortified their dwelling by adding a most luxurious tower and surrounding wall, yet within the church the only reminder we have of them is the tomb recess in the S. wall with their armorial shield over, and perhaps, the enlarged window above. A clear instance of the general pattern whereby funds were diverted into fortified homesteads rather than indefensible churches.

So Edlingham remains today with few alterations to serve its community as it did in the day of the Feltons.

EGLINGHAM. St. Maurice.

Pleasantly placed in one of the most attractive villages in the county, Eglingham impresses at once with its fine tower. Of late 13C aspect, it is built in large stones and so sturdy that the builders did not consider buttresses to be necessary. There are lancet lights, which are paired in the belfry stage with heads cut into a single stone.

Next, the chancel, with an astonishing S. façade of work 17C in date but a survival of medieval basics without a trace of classicism. A visitor seeing a picture of this out of context might well conceive it to be a wing of some pleasant Tudor manor house rather than the chancel of a church. The triple round headed lights on either side of a door with four-centred head, all with straight clasping dripstones, make a composition as charming as it is unexpected. The tower and chancel yield pure enjoyment, but it has to be said that the remainder of the church, though restfully plain, is of such complexity that anyone wishing to unravel it is well advised to consult the Northumberland County History and be prepared to expend a considerable effort! Others may be content to notice the font dated 1663 with enigmatic lettering, and the discarded section of font pedestal with 12C arcading.

ELSDON. St. Cuthbert.

Elsdon lies in a hollow amidst green hills and its houses encircle a wide pleasant green. The surroundings are deeply rural and the modest bell turret of the church leaves us unprepared for the impressive interior. For it at once becomes evident that both nave and transepts are aisled, and the effect of size is increased by the multiplicity of rather narrow arches.

Exterior stonework is of roughly coursed rubble, but the chancel windows on the S. side have flowing 14C tracery. All three differ in size, with the largest at the E. end nearest the altar. In spirit, this recalls Bishop Burnell's rich church at Action Burnell in Shropshire, though the Elsdon façade is crude by comparison. Notice for example the few ill fitting pieces which make up the three light window head, the other two being monolithic. Internally too, the large chancel is extremely plain, with triple sedilia in the form of quite undecorated slots.

The nave holds a shadow of an early church in the W. respond of the arcades which are round half columns with caps and bases of 12C appearance. The aisles are most uncommon, narrow and in the form of a half tunnel vault. That this was not the original intention may be seen in the N. aisle, where corbels for a normal lean-to roof appear beneath the vault crown. There may have been a proposal to vault the nave, as happened at Bellingham, since the aisles have the form of a continuous flying buttress. Although the arcades are severely plain with chamfers rather than mouldings, the second capital from the W. on the S. side has been selected for a little foliage carving, likely to be the work of the master mason, with parallels at Newbiggin, Bamburgh and elsewhere. The blocked arch in the W. gable possibly indicates an unfulfilled scheme to add a tower.

As a whole, Elsdon has the aspect of an ambitious building, lacking in finished masoncraft, as if the means were not quite equal to the intention. And this poses an interesting problem. A church having long transepts with aisles would fall naturally into place in the Tyne Valley in the 13C, but is quite unexpected in remote Northumberland in the 14C. Allowing for powerful patronage from the Umfraville lords of Redesdale, the answer may well be that Elsdon in its present form is a recasting of a 13C church to meet the requirements of the 14C onwards. It is a matter calling for further study but adds an enjoyable dimension to the appreciation of Elsdon church.

EMBLETON. Holy Trinity.

First impressions are likely to be of a High Victorian chancel and a tower with an upper stage having a pierced parapet resembling Thirsk in North Yorkshire. Then a pleasing porch with no upper room (Warkworth is our only example), but with a fine statue niche, now unhappily empty, over the outer door. These are late medieval, and the tower ribbed vault is compatible in style and might reproduce original work. Slit windows indicate an earlier date for the lowest tower stage, and the 13C arcades are of considerable interest. Their arches have a hood with prominent nailhead ornament as in earlier work at Haltwhistle, and another significant detail is that over the capitals there are exceptionally large dogtooth motifs serving as chamfer stops. It has long been known that the same form occurs in the S. arcade at Whittingham, and we may add that the brackets with lobes surmounted by foliage also occur in both buildings. Such individual elements suggest work by the same hand, one of the elusive signs, which may in time reveal something of relevance to the practice and organisation of 13C masoncraft in our area.

The E. end of the N. aisle has been widened to form a small chapel, now rebuilt, separated from the aisle by a low arch which gives almost the feeling of a double aisle. The tracery window in its N. wall is one of the smallest we have in which the head is formed from separate pieces.

The chancel and its arch, dating from 1867, is a striking essay in the Geometrical style. The use of alternating red and light stones in the arch is justified by medieval precedents of Holy Island and Norham, and the whole composition may be looked upon as one of F.R. Wilson's best, even though the period chosen is not one in which major rebuilding schemes were common in Northumberland.

FARNE ISLAND. St. Cuthbert.

A visit to the Farnes should include the chapel on Inner Farne, overlooked by the massive tower house of Prior Castell. There remains but a single rectangular compartment, with the curving 14C tracery of a two-light window cut in one stone and in an advanced state of weathering.

The interior is crowded with spectacular 17C stalls from Durham cathedral, of Bishop Cosin's period, which cannot fail to impress, as in its own way will the memorial window to Grace Darling, so close to the scene of her renowned exploit.

Plate 1 Alwinton. St. Michael. On the fringe of the Cheviots.

Plate 2 Stamfordham. St Mary. A pastoral vale.

Plate 3 Corsenside. St. Cuthbert. The open moor.

Plate 4 Bywell. St Andrew. Tower from N: original divided belfry opening.

Plate 5 Bolam. St Andrew. W. face of tower.

Plate 6 Old Bewick. Holy Trinity. Nave and chancel with apse.

Plate 7 Thockrington. St Aidan: Vaulted chancel with rebuilt nave.

Plate 8 Seaton Delaval. Our Lady. Interior looking E. with twin arches.

Plate 9 Norham. St Cuthbert. Late 12C S. arcade and chancel arch.

Plate 10 Warkworth. St Lawrence. N. nave wall.

Plate 11 Heddon. St Andrew. Chancel interior with vaulted bay.

Plate 12 Alnham. St Michael. Chancel arch looking E.

Plate 13 Newburn. St Michael. Nave N. arcade with later S. arcade.

Plate 14 Haltwhistle. Holy Cross. From S.E.

Plate 15 Ovingham. St Mary. Long lancets of chancel and S. transept from E.

Plate 16 Corbridge. St Andrew. S. chancel wall.

Plate 17 Bamburgh. St Aidan. The impressively large chancel from S.E.

Plate 18 Ovingham. St. Mary. S. arcade with tall and slender round columns.

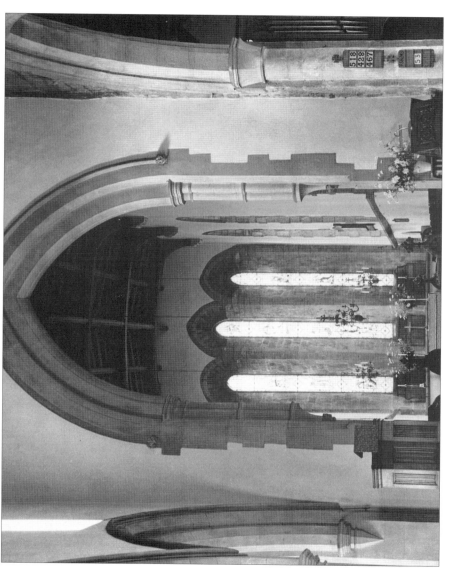

Plate 19 Bywell. St Peter. The chancel interior, deceptively small with elongated E. lancets.

Plate 20 Whalton. St Mary Magdalene.
The unique chancel aisle column with its emphatic dogtooth ornament.

Plate 21 Whalton. St Mary Magdalene. An impression of the 13C interior.

Plate 22 Haltwhistle. Holy Cross. Stepped sedilia with their restrained moulding.

Plate 23 Whalton. St Mary Magdalene. Carved head stops over the S. arcade.

Plate 24 Cambo.
Holy Trinity.
Grave cover with
cross of circlets and
sword.

Plate 25 Newbiggin. St Bartholomew. Richly carved grave cover with delicate flowers, shears and key.

Plate 26 Newbiggin. St Bartholomew. Sited on N. point of the bay.

Plate 27 Newbiggin. St Bartholomew. The nave looking W.

Plate 28 Felton. St Michael. Monolithic tracery.

Plate 29 Morpeth. St Mary. S.E. view of chancel and aisle.

Plate 30 Kirkharle. St Wilfrid.
Chancel interior with sedilia and restored reticulated tracery.

Plate 31 Morpeth. St Mary. 14C sedilia with floral carving and entertaining figures.

Plate 32 Widdrington. Holy Trinity. From S. showing windows with flowing tracery.

Plate 33 Widdrington. Holy Trinity. Nave interior with S. aisle and chapel.

Plate 34 Alnwick. St Michael. Large country town church with fully developed plan.

Plate 35 Alnwick. St Michael.
Carved capital in chancel with vine and angel displaying shield.

Plate 36 Beltingham. St Cuthbert. Undivided chapel with ample windows.

Plate 37 Kirknewton. St Gregory. Chancel with pointed stone vault resembling tower house basement.

Plate 38 Chillingham. St Peter. Table tomb of Sir Ralph Grey, d. 1443, and his wife.

Plate 39 Bothal. St Andrew. Alabaster effigies and table tomb of Ralph Lord Ogle and his wife.

Plate 40 Bothal. St Andrew. Nave roof of about 1500 with angel figures on the ridge.

Plate 41 Ponteland. St Mary. A synthesis of 12C, 13C, 14C and 15C.

Plate 42 Warkworth. St Lawrence. 12C church with added spire and 14C and 15C aisle.

FELTON. St. Michael

Stands on a spur overlooking the village but screened from it by trees, and it has to be sought unexpectedly by a narrow steep lane joining the Swarland road. Then we see a large nave with aisles yet possessing only a bell turret at the W. end, in the common Northumbrian manner. More unusual is the aspect of the nave, which seems to have no roof since its pitch is so flat as hardly to be visible from ground level, in contrast to the high roof of the chancel. Lancets in the W. gable, and a blocked one in the S. wall W. of the porch suggest extensive medieval remains and it soon becomes apparent that Felton has pleasing surprises. The first is encountered when a circuit of the exterior brings us to the E. gable of the S. aisle. For here is a five light window with a tracery head of pure Geometrical design, a rarity in the district, and carved entirely in a single piece of stone six feet wide (*plate 28*). It is when monolithic tracery reaches this size that the technique begins to seem abnormal, though doubtless encouraged by the local prevalence of good freestone. The date is probably about 1330, when a chantry was established by Roger Mauduit, and if so the pattern was then rather obsolete, though an appreciable time lag could be expected for a remote provincial site.

Entry to the church provides the next enjoyable experience, for in addition to the outer and inner porch doors, a third one faces us in a section of wall separating the two parts of the S. arcade. It does not take long to surmise that this is the original S. nave door of about 1200, allowed to remain when the S. aisle was extended to the full length of the nave and the present porch with its rib-vaulted roof added to its outer wall. Nearby is a decorated niche possibly for holy water.

The nave impresses by its large size, about the fourth largest in the county, and with a N. arcade of five bays. The S. aisle is asymmetric. The two E. bays, with wide 14C arches, extend as far as the porch, and were probably built as a chapel. The part of the aisle lying W. of the porch is extremely interesting as it contains capitals and an arch of late 12C appearance. The responds of this arch are dissimilar; one rises from floor level, the other forms in effect an elongated bracket. It is tempting to see this as the upper part of the E. respond of the N. arcade, which changes from round to octagonal half way up. If so, this western part of the aisle was constructed from re-used material derived from other parts of the church. That a 12C chapel originally stood in this position is not impossible, but does seem less likely. A fascinating issue on which to reflect.

The chancel arch also has early concave capitals but these support a high acutely pointed arch, and there are lancet windows of the type with trefoil rere arches. The chancel is short, with proportions differing so much from others of the 13C that it is likely to have been shortened in the course of repair or rebuilding of the E. gable.

A rare monument is the half effigy of a priest in low relief, at present against the N. aisle wall; there is another example in the chancel of Ingram church. Surprises are an appealing element of the churches of Northumberland, and Felton is a fine instance of this characteristic.

FORD. St. Michael

Stands apart from the village, neighbouring the castle, and from its hillside there are extensive views across Glendale to the Cheviots. As calming a place to linger as we could wish, yet with an insecure past recalled by the remains of the vicar's tower house in the adjoining meadow.

Nor is the history of the church at all easy to disentangle, for much is modern. Externally, the bell turret is an important element, and poses a question as to how much of it may go back to the 13C. Possibly, at least the buttress which supports the bell cote itself. Then, at the SE. corner of the aisle, is an elegant diagonal buttress with statue niches, indicating a 14C rather than a 13C date, and probably denoting a widening of the original S. aisle. The chancel is mostly rebuilt.

Within, we find a 13C S. arcade with exceptionally wide arches for its period; it would be fascinating to know how this decision was taken, when four arches of average span would have done the job. One capital bears a double row of nail head ornament, and large heads appear beneath the bracket responds, in a style encountered also at Newbiggin and Woodhorn. So that whatever may have happened subsequently, there was a well-endowed church of quality here in the 13C. And in the floor at the W. end are medieval grave covers, one of which should not be missed, for it is engraved with the outline of an early form of bagpipe.

GUYZANCE. St. Wilfrid.

Or Brainshaugh, where a nunnery was recorded in the 12C, comprises the ruins of a chapel beautifully situated on a spacious level haugh beside the Coquet, and easily seen from the nearby lane. It is difficult to interpret, being now a rectangle of nave and chancel with evidence of a short aisle on the S. side. It has been updated since its foundation and it is rather startling to note a double bowled piscina indicating alterations made at the end of the 13C or beginning of the 14C. There is little other detail and this remains a site requiring a full investigation before an attractive little building can be fitted into its context.

HALTON.

Chapel neighbours the impressive tower with its 17C wing. It is post-medieval except for the chancel arch, of a single square order rising from plainest imposts in a 12C manner. This may even have undergone some reconstruction, but all should enjoy a visit to this light interior amidst its lovely surroundings.

HALTWHISTLE. Holy Cross.

Has been much restored externally, yet this has been done with regard to the original design, so with half closed eyes we can see the church today very much as we would have seen it early in the 13C (*plate 14*). It has lancet windows throughout, with high pitched roof and low aisles, and is an unusually large church to be provided with only a bell turret instead of a tower, in which it resembles Simonburn and contrasts with the transeptal towered churches of the lower Tyne valley. The chancel is now a major component showing the tendency to enlarged clerical staff and more elaborate services, with increasing relegation from the congregation and what we should regard today as secular uses of the nave.

The interior is imposing, if dark, the nave having fine four bay arcades with nail head on the arch hoods. The narrow moulded capitals are interesting, with alternate long and short sides, an evident attempt to match the shape of the chamfered arches, more usually achieved by an octagonal upper surface. The survival of a contemporary clerestory is a rarity, and here the builder has preferred to have the windows over the columns instead of 'void over void' usually accepted as more satisfying to the eye. Here the decision seems sound, due to the high arches, and altogether we appear to be in touch with a master capable of independent thought and prepared to experiment with his bay design.

The large chancel has a fine triple set of sedilia (*plate 22*), with seats of graduated height emphasising the rank of clergy when seated during the extended offices now coming into use. In the chancel floor notice particularly a large double grave cover in exceptionally deep relief.

HARTBURN. St. Andrew.

Hartburn church has a happily rural approach, most of all when the roses bordering the path are in bloom. As we have it today, the church gives a remarkably complete impression of the lancet period of the 13C, yet in doing so it almost certainly effaces the memory of earlier buildings on the site. Thus the lower NE quoins of the nave comprise massive stones, while a careful search above the W. bays of the arcades will reveal several incised saltire crosses, similar to ones at Bolam.

The handsome S. door has double rows of dogtooth continued down to ground level, similarly to the round arched S. door at Bolam, but without the structural flaws of the latter. On the E. jamb is a clearly incised maltese cross and two others, the significance of which has never been satisfactorily explained, though some have suspected a connection with the Knights Templars who had a commandery at Temple Thornton, about one mile distant.

Although aisle walls have been rebuilt and heightened, the arcades remain intact. The second capital from the W. on the S. side is distinguished by a heavy ball ornament, and the first from the E. on the same side has a carved fish, an early Christian symbol which might be linked with the dedication to St. Andrew. A number of grotesque and imaginative hood stops will also be found above the capitals, which have an odd appearance of being too small for the arches. In the NE respond is a small shafted corner piscina, a primitive echo of a kind highly developed and widespread in Norfolk.

The chancel arch is of impressive height and has formerly possessed nook shafts to its jambs though now only the small bases and caps remain. For once, it forms an adequate frame to the immensely long chancel. This appearance is in no way an illusion; the ratio of length to breadth is much greater than other chancels of similar date, so much so that it strongly suggests an extension of the original design. This is confirmed by details of the fabric, for example there are two piscinas, and outside there is a change in the level of the prominent string course and the shape of the S. lancets. The triplet at the E. end are separated by buttresses which change from square to octagonal plan at half height, a feature which probably originated at the priories of Brinkburn and Hexham and is found also at Ovingham. The priest's door has a shouldered lintel as at Meldon and Rothbury, and there is a triple set of sedilia enhanced by shafts and restrained mouldings which contrast with the totally different concept of the 14C set at Morpeth.

It remains to notice some curious changes at the W. end. In the W. wall of the tower a fine three light window with Perpendicular panel tracery has been inserted. The tracery is carved in a single stone, but though it has a pointed shape, the stone in which it is carved is rectangular, perhaps for strength and to give less trouble fitting into the wall courses. When this window was filled with coloured glass, it would have given a fine appearance to the W. end of the church seen through the tall tower arch. But then came the decision to render the tower secure and fireproof by inserting a vault, with the necessity of blocking up the tower arch, so that now the window lights only the tower basement. Somewhat similar sequences are to be found at Kirkwhelpington and Newbiggin.

HAYDON BRIDGE.

The way to the old church of Haydon lies up a winding lane climbing the steep hillside north of the village, with delightful views across the Tyne valley towards Langley. And there we find the chancel, only, of the lonely church. The short widely spaced triplet lancets of its E. end have round heads in the 12C manner, and make an interesting comparison with Bellingham, where the aspect is similar but the heads are pointed. Inside, one has the strange sight of a Roman altar shaped into a font, and on the N. side the blocking of a door is completely made up of medieval grave cover fragments. A miniature carved figure with an elaborate canopy seems to derive from the 14C and calls to mind a similar piece at Corsenside. The small S. chapel has a narrow window with quite elaborate, if cramped, tracery worked in a single stone.

HEDDON. St. Andrew.

When you leave the A69 slip road and make towards the village of Heddon, St. Andrew's is seen ahead in a grove of trees surmounting a knoll. It is a place of many architectural pleasures. To encourage enjoyment, it is probably best to look first at the SE external corner of the nave against which the S. aisle gable is built with a straight joint Here one sees huge corner stones, irregularly narrow and wide, and though one face is covered, this is accepted as evidence of a former Anglo-Saxon church, though its precise form is not established by the remains above ground.

It is best next to view the chancel interior and admire the opulent Norman of its eastern half (*plate 11*). For here is an early ribbed quadripartite vault inevitably setting the mind towards Durham and denoting skills not usually available for parish church construction. The transept arch has become distorted in shape; it is inadequately supported by the chancel walls. All the arch stones are decorated with horizontal zigzag. In the county this is only to be compared with Warkworth, but in Newcastle similar work is found in the chapel of the castle. The W. half of the chancel is quite plain, perhaps speaking to an unfulfilled intention for a second vaulted compartment, but eventually updated by addition of the high pointed 13C arch.

The nave arcades carry the story further. On the N. side the capitals of the E. arch have elaborate late 12C carving differing so much from local style as to pose a question regarding their source. Notice that the S. arcade is in the later 13C manner, matching the W. arch on the N. side. The implication is that addition of the S. aisle and extension of the nave were planned as one operation, quite possibly because the Anglo Saxon nave was found to be too small. Late in the 13C, the chancel windows were altered. Externally, they are seen as a close pair of lancets, the space between their tops being decorated by small openings containing heads, which are doubtfully original. Internally, each pair of lancets is gathered under a single arch, the sill of the E. pair being continued downwards to provide an undivided seat. At Warden an earlier phase with plain space between the heads is found in the N. transept, while a more confident treatment with carved heads under a single arch occurs at Aydon castle near Corbridge about 1295. At Ryton on the south bank the space is almost pierced to form the immediate forerunner of tracery. Taken together, the group illustrates active development of window design in the Tyne valley at the end of the 13C.

HOLY ISLAND. St. Mary.

If one wished to gain an impression of a typical Northumbrian village church of the 13C, Holy Island with its long lancet chancel, nave with narrow aisles and bell turret would be a fair example to take. Three bays of the N. arcade with round arches belong stylistically to the late 12C and so appear to antedate the chancel. The latter is above the average elongation for its period, and the lancet windows with the graded triplet at the E. end are well proportioned if austere. The chancel arch is wide with no capitals and of rather crude build. It evidently replaces an earlier narrow arch of which a trace is now exposed above its crown. This provides a contrast to Bamburgh where the arch seems inadequate to the splendid chancel. The Holy Island arches are also built in alternate light and dark stone as found at Norham. No doubt the availability of both types of stone on the island prompted the builder's thoughts in this direction; the result calls to mind the Northamptonshire group including Irthlingbrough, Woodford and Farndish. Today it seems an acquired taste like the polychrome work of the Victorian era. Yet in its time, allowing the stones to speak in this way must have appeared not only innovative but even restrained amidst the vivid colour painting on plaster, which was then so general.

The short arch at the W. end of the N. arcade looks odd, and seems to be in some way connected with the addition of the S. aisle, which it matches in detail. The usual explanation is that when the S. aisle was added the nave was lengthened towards the W. and the N. arcade extended to match with a short bay. But it is possible that the need was actually to shorten the nave, because the ground falls away steeply outside and there may have been structural failure. Even today, the W. responds may be seen to lean quite visibly. There can never have been any possibility of a W. tower, and the bell turret itself is carried on a tall lightly built arch.

One pleasing feature of the church is unhappily missing. Those seemingly wide lancets in the S. aisle wall are known from old pictures to have been fitted with flowing tracery in 14C style; no doubt they became weathered by sea air beyond hope of renewal. The 20th century has made its own tribute in the glowing needlework carpet beyond the altar rails.

HOLYSTONE. St. Mary.

The appealing little church is tucked away behind the hamlet, beside the road leading to the Forestry car park, at the edge of a vast moorland landscape. There is known to have been hereabouts a house of Augustinian nuns which, not surprisingly, suffered from great privations due to its proximity to the border. It is hard to picture today, and very little of the middle ages is to be seen in the church. Only at the S. gate, and in a low position pointing to a change of level, is the capital and respond of a former arch. The nave is thought to have occupied the position of the chancel of an earlier church, and to this may belong a few lower courses of masonry with embedded sills of windows in the S. wall. Three grave covers of good design nearby, and sadly weathering away, are indications of the existence of a medieval community.

ILDERTON. St. Michael

Even more remote in the Cheviot foothills than Kirknewton, Ilderton offers for medieval study only the sturdy W. tower of late 13C date, with a rugged aspect appropriate to its environment. It has double buttresses clasping the W. corners, and its basement is on a curiously lower level than the present nave floor, so that the tower arch is shortened as seen from the interior. It may be that the rebuilt nave is raised upon earlier walls, and it is well worth entering to see the dignified series of memorial tablets on the N. and W. walls.

INGRAM. St. Michael.

Ingram church is delightfully situated at the point where the Breamish leaves the hills to form a series of meanders over the wide level valley, where its tower seems to beckon to us from the trees across the stream.

A closer view discloses little that is medieval in the exterior except for the tower. This was in fact rebuilt about 1890 with numbered stones so that an exact replica was secured, the base course being possibly undisturbed. Without buttresses and with slit windows, the regular courses and quoins are in a Norman manner, but the original date remains problematical. Internally, however, the tower arch with its two flush orders corresponds more clearly to an 11C origin.

With the nave arcades we are clearly in the 13C, a plain but well proportioned design with conspicuous examples of the long capital, and a matching chancel arch with wide soaring arch on low responds. On a bracket nearby is the pleasing surprise of a pair of carved leaves, not perhaps of a high art form, but aspiring to it. Altogether there is a notable resemblance to the nave of Whalton church, including the moulded bases of the columns, which here are closer to floor level.

A strange feature is that the arcades come to a stop before reaching the chancel arch, leaving an enigmatic gap in the composition. It may be that part of an early church remained here because it was intended to add or rebuild chapels at this point. And the E. imposts of the S. arch are archaic with their deep hollow moulding, though not necessarily in situ, a point emphasised by the strange appearance of a sundial on the interior. It is known that medieval aisle chapels existed, that their arches and the nave arcades were blocked before 1870, and that modern aisle walls were added to accompany the cleared arches. Part of the building history is thus shrouded in complexity.

A hint of medieval status is to be found in the fragment of a low relief effigy of a figure in ecclesiastical dress built into the N. chancel wall, similar to a slab in Felton church. The font has an attractive bowl dated 1662, a panelled octagon with carved motifs including foliage and crescents.

KIRKHARLE. St. Wilfrid.

The church is seen across the meadows from the A696, though it may be doubted whether it is glimpsed by many visitors speeding along this busy highway. Yet to thread the tiny hamlet and reach the churchyard offers a peaceful retreat.

What we find is a surprisingly uniform display of 14C style, with reticulated tracery to the windows. So far as the nave is concerned this work is modern, and so is the tracery of the S. chancel windows, but these may be seen to be close reproductions of the original ones on the N. side, which go with the priest's door and the low side windows. This chancel is of remarkably compact design, and the way in which a fine set of sedilia is incorporated in a relatively small space without disturbing the layout is admirable (*plate 30*). It is interesting to see how the builder has incorporated all the facilities of the larger chancel of Morpeth whilst avoiding the unsymmetrical awkwardness of windows and priest's door so evident there.

The chancel arch is wide and tall and has no capitals, the arch simply dying into the responds as at Rothbury. There are records of chantry foundations in the church, but no evidence of aisles, so the space on either side of the chancel arch has been used to house altars. Examination of the walls will reveal an unusually numerous and varied series of mason marks.

The impressive font formerly belonged to the demolished Newcastle church of All Hallows, and is of the distinctive pattern seen today in St. Nicholas cathedral. The faces of the octagonal bowl are deeply concave and each holds a shield bearing the charge or merchant mark of a notable city family. Although battered and worn, it still conveys to the imagination the lustre of late medieval display.

This appealing little building in a locally scarce style is especially worth a visit.

KIRKNEWTON. St. Gregory.

Stands in its peaceful churchyard deep in the northern foothills of the Cheviots, and from outside looks entirely of recent rebuilding. But inside there are the clearest signs of a troubled medieval past and it is with something approaching a shock that we see the chancel with low pointed barrel vault looking like the basement of a pele tower, and doubtless built by those familiar with such work (*plate 37*). The risk attached to public assembly in this remote part of the border in 1436 was so great that a papal dispensation was granted to allow celebration of mass in any other suitable place in the parish. The evident intention of the parishioners was that part of the building, at least, should be indestructible. Also vaulted is the small S. chapel or Burrell porch housing a rare incised slab of 1458.

The original 13C nave was of fair size and had a N. aisle but was completely rebuilt in the 19C. The square jambs of the exceptionally narrow chancel arch may be the earliest part of the fabric now standing. There is also a link with the early history of the site in the carved panel near its N. respond, with relief figures evidently depicting an epiphany. It has been variously dated as pre-Conquest to early 12C.

In recent years, the perhaps sombre appearance of the interior of St. Gregory's has been lightened by skilful and attractive floral decorations, which would have surprised, and we hope delighted, the medieval builders.

KIRKWHELPINGTON. St. Bartholomew.

Presents an unusual appearance today, long and narrow without aisles and with some curiously domestic looking windows. Only the squat tower looks medieval, with buttresses seemingly applied at random wherever a structural defect appeared. There remains a fine arch to the nave, pointed with a double row of vertical zigzag, though blocked when the tower was strengthened and its basement vaulted. For the rest, it becomes apparent that the most important aspect of St. Bartholomew's is the part which is not there, but which can be pictured from isolated features remaining from the 13C. Thus the S. nave doorway, its pointed arch with deep double roll mouldings, is a form having an antecedent in the round arched S. door at Ovingham, and a development in the S. door at Widdrington. Then, the wide soaring chancel arch on low responds resembling Whalton and Ingram. Moreover the drainage trench outside on the S. reveals a column base implying an aisle to the nave, and also the stylish chamfered double plinth and narrow buttresses of the former elegant chancel. With those go the double sedilia having a delicate column separating the two seats. Transept foundations have been uncovered, though their relation to the other remains is not fully determined. So the later history of ruin and curtailment has deprived us of what must have been a notable monument to the 13C art of Northumberland.

It is all the more agreeable to find a rather basic but still handsome wooden pulpit and sounding board of the 18C.

LESBURY. St. Mary.

Lesbury church, pleasantly sited at the east end of the village, appears from the outside to be very much rebuilt, and so it is, although the tower is medieval, and quite possibly 12C in its lower courses. Our interest is quickened on entering by the sight of a N. aisle with an arcade in the style of the late 12C with concave capitals having square abaci. It is of two bays only, as at Widdrington but with a deep wing at either end. Further, this aisle is continued along the N. wall of the chancel, an early example of a plan seen also at Rothbury, Whalton and Corbridge. At least one of the E. arches is known to have been altered but there is no reason to doubt that the development belongs to the 12C. The narrow pointed chancel arch fits badly onto its jambs and imposts, which are likely to be earlier. Lack of abutment due to the aisle on the N. side may have counselled the builders against widening.

Fragments incorporated in renewed lancet windows suggest some 13C updating, and the tower may have been heightened to contain the extremely high arch. The N. chancel wall has a Perpendicular style window with three cusped heads shaped from a single large stone. However as at Edlingham, there was no addition of a S. aisle and this may be a sign of a static or declining community; Lesbury was originally the mother church of the lower Aln valley, Alnwick and Alnmouth being chapelries, a status almost completely reversed by the end of the middle ages.

The font is an interesting one with concave sides in the Newcastle manner, bearing Percy family symbols of lockets and crescents.

LONGFRAMLINGTON. St. Mary.

A small nave and chancel church looking today very much as it must have done when newly built in the late 12C, for it has never required enlargement. And it has two features of architectural delight. One is the S. door, with an arch in three square orders supported by water leaf capitals typical of their period, an ambitious entry to a building of simple external appearance. The other is the chancel arch, of similar design, but whose arch orders seem to float almost casually on slender columns completely separated from the wall, so that you can pass a hand behind them. These arches cause one to realise how very pleasing in appearance was the round arched style in its latest development, and almost to regret the intrusion of the pointed arch which could appear quite stark in appearance until it was eventually softened by extensive deep mouldings and carved capitals.

The accomplishment of this work seems more than could be expected from a local contractor or journeyman mason and renders it most probable that we see here the hand of those engaged at major sites such as Newminster, or possibly at Brinkburn where similar design can be found in the triforium of the transepts.

Although the plan of the church was not extended, it would seem that larger windows were contemplated at a later date, for in the N. chancel wall is a twin light with a 14C tracery head cut from one stone in the preferred local manner.

LONGHOUGHTON. St. Peter.

The tower of Longhoughton surely fulfils the expectation of what a Norman tower should be like. Massive, with thick walls, it dominates the approach along the churchyard path. It is not quite homogeneous, for the lower part is in a reddish stone, the upper part a lighter grey, as if some factor has led to a change of quarry, perhaps during a pause in building or exhaustion of one of the supplies. Internally, high interest attaches to the tower arch and the chancel arch, and to the surprising difference between them. The chancel arch is narrow, square and lacking even a chamfer, with patches of rubble core visible in the arch itself. It looks archaic, seeming to group with Birtley and Corsenside, yet lacking details which might establish a pre-Conquest date. The tower arch is wide and tall with roll mouldings to the arch, evidently built when funds and skills were more readily available. Even so, it rests on plain square responds without shafts, which hardly form an adequate match, and leave it without a downward continuation such as is seen at Norham.

The S. aisle has an arcade of familiar north country 13C style, springing from brackets at each end. Originally the E. gable housed a single lancet, of which the blocked head remains visible externally, but this was replaced later by a 14C twin light with foiled heads and a tracery panel carved in shallow relief, as found in some windows in Belsay castle. On the S. side of the chancel arch is a low opening of the kind termed a squint, providing an alternative view towards the main altar. The chancel at Longhoughton, like that at Alnham, shows an early stage of enlargement from the small but more intimate choir and sanctuary of earlier 12C years.

MELDON. St. John.

This small aisleless church with no structural division between nave and chancel is worthy of being classed as a gem of its kind. Although accepted as a parish church, it must always have served a small community, and set amongst deeply rural surroundings, it is a place where time seems to lose its meaning. The walls contain many reddened stones, as in the N. chancel wall at Mitford, and patches of rough irregular masonry may be re-used from an earlier building. Nevertheless, the church as we have it today is in the style of the late 13C, though with many signs of gentle restoration. The charming priest's door with its shouldered lintel or 'Caernarfon' arch must look much as it always has done, resembling those at Hartburn and Rothbury, and the pointed door to the nave faces a similar, better preserved one on the N. side, opening now to a vestry. The chancel is marked only by a wooden screen, no doubt standing in the position of its medieval predecessors. In the SE. corner, where a small lancet adjoins the priest's door, is a delicate pillar piscina with a pointed niche over. Only the frame of the E. window is original and possibly designed for grouped lancets; it now has some attractive insets of modern coloured glass set in a plain surround carefully modulated by ribbed structure. The earlier armorial glass in the S. lancets is also pleasing and worthy of inspection.

At the W. end is an effigy of a squire in mid 17C armour, the head resting awkwardly on the left arm in the way dubbed the 'toothache' style. The tradition is that he represents Sir Wm. Fenwick, husband of the notorious Meg of Meldon whose portrait may be seen today at Doddington Hall, Lincs. The attribution is uncertain though his dates would be consistent with the type of armour depicted.

MITFORD. St. Mary Magdalene.

Mitford church has as delightful a setting as could be wished, neighboured by the castle ruins and, closer at hand, a fragment of the old manor house bearing the date 1637. The church itself has been one of magnificence, much of which has survived. There is a hint of it in the creditable Victorian tower and spire, but it is seen to full effect in the splendid chancel of the early 13C, one of the largest of its period in the county. The lancet windows are not so long as found in the Tyne valley, but form an imposing row rendered grammatical by deeply projecting buttresses with emphatic string and base courses. A low side window and a priest's door fit naturally into the façade, yet the door has a curious feature perhaps offering a sidelight on the medieval mind, for its pointed head is made of pieces of 12C zigzag evidently intended for a round arch. Determination to use these fragments has only just avoided spoiling a masterly overall design.

On the way to the nave door we pass a small transept of contrasting plainness, with a two light 14C window of cusped ogee heads between which is a shield bearing three moles for Mitford of Molesden.

When we enter the church the importance of an earlier building scheme becomes evident, for on the S. is an arcade of massive Norman columns surmounted by round moulded arches with scalloped capitals and heavy square bases ornamented with spurs at the corners. The appearance of this work is perhaps unnaturally smooth and clear cut due to the arches being re-surfaced after they were walled up when the ground plan was contracted. There was at least a chapel on the N. side, with foliage carving on vertical sectors of a remaining capital, though on this side there are abundant signs of damage and repair, with fire reddened stones. Even this does not reveal the full extent of the Norman church, for close examination of the E. end of the S. aisle shows a shaft implying an arch into a former apse. No doubt a chancel in keeping with the nave was planned, though it must soon have been replaced by the present one and perhaps may not have been completed. Its main impression now is of spaciousness, enhanced by simple shafted sedilia and piscina. One may indeed wonder at the scale of the work at Mitford, reflecting probably the resources of the Bertram family, founders of Brinkburn priory and patrons of nearby Newminster Abbey. That so much should have survived the havoc and poverty of the late Middle Ages in Northumberland is most fortunate.

MORPETH. St. Mary.

The visitor to Morpeth St. Mary (*plate 29*), may feel surprise at finding a Northumbrian church, which looks entirely of the 14C, the more so because it does not show any clear signs of the 13C. Yet only two miles to the west is the large lancet chancel of Mitford, a church which in its original form was larger even than Morpeth. The position of St. Mary's is also strange, half a mile south of the old town by the bridge, perhaps to be explained by close proximity to the castle. Lacking the patronage of a distinguished local lord as at Mitford, its development may reflect a late medieval prosperity of Morpeth town.

This impression of a prosperous town church is heightened on entering, when we are greeted by a spacious nave with wide aisles separated by arcades of five bays. There is a tomb recess in the S. aisle and a large squint looking into the chancel on the N. side of the arch. Traces of coloured pattern appear on some columns of the N. arcade. The basement of the low tower is vaulted but opens into the nave by a wide arch. A closer study of the aisle windows will disclose that they are not of uniform build; one type has monolithic tracery set towards the outer wall face; the other has jointed tracery set close to the wall centre. The plan too, is irregular, the two W. bays being narrower and the S. arcade converging towards the W. Although difficult to interpret, these variations point to more than one stage in the building of the nave.

The E. respond of the S. arcade has oak leaf carving, and when visitors who know Patrington church in East Yorkshire enter the chancel, they may notice something familiar in the ornate sedilia with their nodding canopies (*plate 31*). Embedded in these are delicate flowers suggestive of wild rose and globeflower. In complete contrast, though characteristic of their age, are the engaging little figures between. An unusual aumbry door on the N. side is in halves hinged down the centre, and has original iron hinges as does the priest's door on the S. side. The great feature of the chancel is the magnificent E. window, skilfully restored and retaining perhaps two thirds of the original glass. The main lights form a complete Jesse tree; the branches made up of Old Testament prophets each carrying a scroll with words foretelling the coming of Christ. Scenes from the life of the Virgin Mary appropriately occupy the tracery lights. Here we see something of the colour of the 14C church and the way in which its stories and doctrine were conveyed quite literally by colour transparencies. Nor is this all, for the tracery lights of the S. aisle E. window have contemporary glass portraying the Lord with St. Blaize and St. Denis.

In leaving, look again at the outside of this impressive chancel with its statue niches. The walls are beautifully laid in regular courses with fine joints, and one of the few places where we may see masonry of comparable quality is in the tower of Edlingham castle. Only after some time does it strike one that the design is perhaps not fully successful – the division into bays is upset by the window spacing, short then long, and in part this is due to the decorative sedilia and to the window sills being brought below the level of the priest's door head. The problem is a recurrent one. Thus at Framlingham in Suffolk the door is behind a cutaway buttress, at Trunch in Norfolk it is built into the buttress and at Sleaford in Lincolnshire it projects boldly into the adjoining window. A visit to Kirkharle will show how a brilliant designer achieved a neat solution in a relatively small façade.

NETHERWITTON. St. Giles.

Approached from the village, sheltered amongst trees on the edge of the hall grounds, Netherwitton may seem a strange inclusion in a survey of medieval churches, having been comprehensively rebuilt in the 18C and 19C. But the charming building has been Gothicised and retains the effigy of a 14C lady. This was rescued from the foundations when the aisle was built and though worn has been of high quality, her gown being charged with what appears to be a heraldic trellis or 'fret.'

NEWBIGGIN. St. Bartholomew.

Has perhaps the most dramatic situation of any parish church in Northumberland, far out on a rocky point commanding a wide bay, and perilously close to the waves (*plate 26*). It is a building of impressive length and although there is much evidence of restoration, the bar tracery windows of the chancel give an indication of what will be found within. The small much weathered tower is medieval, and so is the rather dumpy spire, which makes a bland and artless junction with the square tower. The belfry windows have rudimentary intended tracery, but the heads, in either one or two pieces, are not actually pierced. The whole unit was probably intended as a landmark for ships approaching the little harbour of medieval days.

On entering the church we immediately encounter the experience of the full length of the nave, only a little shorter than Alnwick or Warkworth, and with six arches on each side, the largest number in any complete aisle outside of Newcastle (*plate 27*). The four eastern arches are of the 13C, one capital having primitive foliage carving, and they differ from the two later western arches in width and in detail of capitals and bases. The capital of the second pillar from the W. differs on its E. and W. sides, so marking the junction. Both the medieval aisles fell into ruin and that on the S. was never rebuilt, the arches still being blocked by an encasing wall. Even so, the long arcades carry the eye emphatically to the E. chancel window, a fine and rare grouping of five lancets under a single arch, now filled with attractive glass of about 1950. This chancel is remarkably spacious and well lighted, though with a conspicuously plain interior. The sedilia, for example, are formed simply by lowering the sill of a S. window, as at Heddon and Widdrington, and are totally devoid of decoration. The chancel is of the same width as the nave and it is debatable whether there was an arch, for the present one is placed one bay E. of the nave and dates from 1897.

Newbiggin houses a precious display of medieval art in the form of a series of large grave covers, the best and most complete of which are built into the walls of the modern N. aisle, though a few are to be found in the porch. They probably range from early 13C to early 14C in date, after which effigies began to appear in Northumberland. The delicate flowers found on the slab behind the aisle altar are particularly touching, and the high standard of carving denotes an expensive monument of its class (*plate 25*).

Newbiggin occupies a key place in the county's sequence of medieval churches in that it was completed just at the beginning of the disastrous wars of Scottish succession, when funds were increasingly diverted from church maintenance, and so it shows what the development of church building locally might have been like if this disaster had not occurred. Its later history is a sad one of near ruin, with aisles removed and chancel standing roofless, and it is indeed fortunate that so much survives today, enhanced by pleasing light modern furnishings and kneelers with themes of the fishing industry with which it has been associated for so long.

As a chapel of ease, Newbiggin overshadowed the mother church of Woodhorn, as Alnwick did Lesbury, and for this we must probably look to the small pocket of wealth surrounding the active medieval port, and to the donors represented by that handsome series of grave covers. The sea is never far from our thoughts in the church, for always within there is the soft background of the wash of waves round the point.

NEWBURN. St. Michael.

Newburn church stands in a commanding position looking down upon the Tyne valley, and is a large building with much to reward an enquiring visitor. The substantial tower, though superficially recalling the pre-Conquest towers of the upper valley, has regularly coursed masonry and quoins, with twin belfry windows having their heads recessed behind the arch opening, and so inviting a 12C date. Inside, the aisle arcades draw attention (*plate 13*). That on the N. has unchamfered round arches supported by quite slim round columns. The shallow capitals have square abaci and lush water leaf carving reminiscent of those in Durham cathedral Galilee, and pointing to a late 12C date. They look less primitive than the arches, and the transition from arch to round column is here managed with a high degree of skill affording distinct pleasure to the eye. The S. aisle arcade is clearly later, with acutely pointed and chamfered arches supported by alternately round and octagonal pillars, an intermediate design found in several Durham churches such as Ryton but also as far away as Soham and Long Sutton in the Fenland district. We notice how the octagonal abacus fits the join with the chamfered arch and how the logical continuation is to make the column also octagonal. The long 13C chancel has renewed openings, but a relatively late 13C date is suggested by the bar tracery E. window and deep buttresses. Finally the S. aisle was widened to form a transeptal chapel, with angled buttresses and Perpendicular windows, quite a different development from the long 13C transepts of the upper valley and another of the details in which Newburn shows some affinity with churches on the south side of the Tyne.

The altar has an interesting reredos in the form of a painted triptych with doors, brought from Italy in the last decade of the 19C.

NORHAM. St. Cuthbert.

Norham church presents an appearance of unexpected size for the district, far exceeding the parochial needs or resources. The special reason is to be found in the nearby castle of the Bishops of Durham, who were frequently in residence, for St. Cuthbert's, when it was built, was within an outlying part of the Palatinate.

The chancel shows one of the largest expanses of Norman masonry to be seen locally, apart from the great early castles. Especially striking is the row of round headed windows, quite large in themselves, though small in relation to the wall area, and effectively edged with zigzag ornament. A handsome base course with a double roll moulding fittingly endorses the quality of design. The former existence of an apse can be detected near the E. end, but this has been reconstructed as a square bay with a 14C two-light tracery window to illuminate the altar. The rather undistinguished tower is Victorian of about 1850.

The interior is spacious and impressive (*plate 9*). Although only the S. arcade and chancel with its arch are original Norman work it is possible to feel the grandeur of the complete church. That it belongs to the latter part of the 12C is shown by the water leaf capitals and also by the confident strength of the chancel arch with its three members or orders, and its width showing how a stable round arch had at last been achieved. As at St. Mary's Holy Island there are alternate red stones in the arch. Although it is known that there was a Norman N. aisle, the use of uniformly octagonal columns in its restored arcade is perhaps open to question. Walter de la Mare in his disturbing story entitled 'All Hallows' says of his cathedral "The stone piers carried their round arches with an almost intimidating impassivity." – surely also an apt description of the interior of Norham.

Such a building had no need of extension, but one handsome addition of the later middle ages is the elaborate tomb recess in the S. chancel wall, with the effigy of an unidentified early 14C knight. Post medieval furnishings include a pulpit of the17C Durham school and carved Royal Arms of Charles II.

OLD BEWICK. Holy Trinity.

Is only approached by a narrow lane off the Alnwick to Wooler road, easily missed though marked by a modern wayside cross. It leads to the idyllic little glen in which the Norman church (*plate 6*) lies concealed beneath the Chillingham sandstone ridge, looking across to the rounded Cheviot Hills.

From without, the rugged building shows some modern windows, but in the N. wall is a primitive round-headed light and near it a re-used stone with a slot, one of several found in the walls, probably originally anchorages for such a feature as an altar screen, and evidence for a previous church at the site. The S. choir wall has a window with deeply cusped head in a single stone, but the main excitement lies in the apsidal E. end, or rather, half end, for late medieval repairers showed no patience with rounded walls or half dome roofs and squared off the upper part, carrying the corners on projecting squinch arches.

Entering the church is almost a step into the 12C. Here is the basic Norman plan of nave, choir and sanctuary, the semicircular end ideally displaying the altar, and probably quite incidentally forming a good acoustic reflector for the voice. Decoration of the two arches is subdued, comprising mainly billet with some sunk star and cable, but the N. capital has grotesque heads, with menacing teeth and pointed ears like a cat.

To later years belong a few grave covers gathered at the W. end, one of which has a branched stem, and the worn effigy of a lady in the choir. This has been of fine workmanship, shown for instance in the folds of the dress, and has resemblances to the better-preserved lady's effigy at Alnwick. We may wonder which distinguished person came to rest in this remote chapelry of Eglingham.

The Norman experience afforded by Old Bewick is of a rare quality, to be found otherwise only at Seaton Delaval and perhaps Thockrington. This is partly due to intelligent restoration, for the building was roofless and approaching ruin when rescued in the 1860s. For such an unusual conservation we can only feel profoundly thankful.

OVINGHAM. St. Mary.

Ovingham church not only impresses by its size, but when viewed from the churchyard also shows us the main phases of its building history. This falls into two periods, Anglo-Saxon and 13C. To the former belongs the W. tower, our largest example of the class, unbuttressed and with its belfry windows divided by mid-wall shafts and enclosed by the distinctive hood mould found at Bywell and at Billingham in Co. Durham. To the later period belongs almost the whole remaining part of the church, with its long aisled transepts and array of lancet windows of that strikingly elongated kind characteristic of the Tyne valley. They are especially well seen from the SE., from the road, which bends closely round the E. end of the church (*plate 15*). Both transepts have W. aisles so that on entering there are impressive vistas of columns and arches dominating the nave. It seems that unbalanced thrust from the transept arcades has necessitated rebuilding of the two eastern pillars, as these are octagonal and one has a carved capital in a 14C style. The remaining columns are round and remarkably tall (*plate 18*), so it may be that in this characteristic we see a fossil of the earlier Anglo Saxon high walled nave. The chancel is rather short and plain, with a less usual pair of sedilia instead of triplet. By taking up a position in the S. transept we see a virtual forest of arches, and can appreciate the size and completeness of the building. A charming detail is the bracket respond of the transept arcade with its vertical dogtooth strips between shafts, as in the font pedestal of Hexham Abbey and the notable column in Whalton church.

It is evident that considerable wealth has been involved here and also exceptional architectural ambition. Those long transepts, for instance, would not be required in the 13C for chantry altars, as they might have been in the later Middle Ages. But such transepts were needed in the greater monastic churches and it is hard to resist the conclusion that the patrons of Ovingham were inspired to plan their church in a similar way. A connection with the Hexham tradition of masonry is suggested by the elegant buttresses between the E. chancel lancets, changing from square to semi-octagonal in their upper parts. Ovingham is also likely to be the earliest of the major 13C rebuildings near Hexham, to judge by the shallow pilaster buttresses of the S. chancel wall, the round rere arches of some of the lancets, and the S. door with its round arch of double roll mouldings.

The interior is furnished in a subdued manner, and there is an exquisite design of modern coloured glass in the chancel low side window by L.C. Evetts forming a worthy continuation of the art of the middle ages.

PONTELAND. St. Mary.

Is a church of prosperous appearance, which presents an unusually complete sequence of modification and improvement (*plate 41*). This indeed extends beyond the visible remains, as recent excavation has partly confirmed a multi-apsidal configuration. The visible sequence, which is well seen from the outside, begins with the W. tower and its fine Norman W. door with two orders of chevron comprising the arch voussoirs. Its surrounding masonry does not conform to the wall courses, as if it was an afterthought, but the squat thick walled tower lacks clear indication of date and its upper stages may be medieval re-modelling.

The 13C church had a N. transept with admirable tall narrow lancets, showing an affinity with the Tyne valley school of design, of which it may be said to occupy a northern fringe. The chancel too belongs to that period, although with E. and S. windows replaced in the 14C. Those in the S. wall are a handsome set with conventional tracery, but the E. window has a strange combination of stiff rayed circle with flowing flame shaped motifs, an uncomfortable mixture of styles within one head.

In the S. transept we find Perpendicular windows, and also in the wide S. aisle. These latter have four-centred heads with cusps but no tracery, and they closely resemble windows of similar date in the Newcastle churches, notably St. John's; they could well be the work of Newcastle masons. The porch abuts this aisle with a stone slab roof resting on vault ribs, and it now projects beyond the W. wall of the aisle, having apparently been moved from its original position to allow more room for the windows of the new aisle. This makes an interesting comparison with Felton, where the earlier porch was absorbed into the aisle, and with Corbridge, where it was thought best to avoid the problem altogether, for there the S. aisle stops short of the Norman S. door.

Inside, the N. arcade of 1861 has little to detain us, but the S. arcade stands apart with its high bases and arches dying into the columns without capitals, a feature again familiar from the Newcastle churches. Perhaps few would find the appearance of such arches appealing to the eye, as our aesthetic sense seems to prefer some punctuation, and in due course the fashion passed. This arcade possibly dates from the end of the 14C. From the 13C, the long lancets of the N. transept are well displayed; the chancel arch is wide and carried on curious brackets with double carved heads suggestive of Adam and Eve, though much reworked. In the chancel is a handsome trefoil shaped piscina edged, one might almost say embroidered, with dogtooth ornament. The heads of the windows contain some attractive medieval glass including a coat of arms, a bishop's head, chalices and delicious castles going round corners.

ROCK. St. Philip and St. James.

The small chapel of ease to Embleton stands at the end of the main street in one of the most attractive hamlets in Northumberland. Its 12C character is at once declared by the W. door with shafted jambs and chevron ornament to the arch. The S. nave wall too, with shallow pilasters joined by a parapet supported on corbels is of the essence of Norman design, and this is happily enhanced when on entering the door one is faced by a truly splendid chancel arch with deep horizontal zigzag, springing from cushion capitals. Over it is a recently disclosed string course with dentil ornament. The modern apsidal sanctuary beyond is at least sufficiently in keeping as not to upset appreciation of the arch. On the other hand one could wish it had not been found necessary to add a 19C N. aisle to house a disproportionately large organ, for the chapel itself had served the middle ages without alteration to its plan. The N. aisle wall does however include a re-erected 12C slit window.

ROTHBURY. All Saints.

Rothbury church has a good Victorian W. tower of 1850 which provides a focus for the E. end of the village green and may be glimpsed from many surrounding points of view, including the grounds of Cragside, while the sound of its clock chimes ranges far and wide over the valley.

That said, it is impossible to view without a feeling of regret the little that remains of a 13C building or to note the loss of a pre-Conquest one which remote sensing suggests may have extended westwards under the roadway. An archaic tower is known from early pictures, but all that can be seen of the period is the carved section of Anglo-Saxon cross now supporting the font basin. For the rest, there is only the 13C chancel, with the arcade of its N. chapel. This chancel has much architectural interest. There is a pleasing priest's door with shouldered lintel, resembling those at Hartburn and Meldon. Two scratch dials are found on and near one of the deep buttresses with offsets, which seem to be an addition to the original design. The E. window is a fascinating example of how close together you can place three lancets without enclosing them under one arch, and may be compared with Bolam, where there is an arch on the inside only, and Newbiggin, where a complete unity has finally been achieved.

Inside, the chancel arch, of quite astonishing height and without capitals perhaps derives its appearance from the Newcastle churches. Then on the S.

interior is an ample aumbry with triple head combined with a piscina. Most of the details point to a date late in the 13C when builders were beginning to free themselves from the constraints of the lancet style which had dominated church building for so long. Little remains to disclose the form of the N. chancel chapel save the two arches which separate it from the choir. Very evident between them is the 18C Thomlinson monument with its gilded cherubs heads, perhaps not highly refined art yet effective in display.

A vestige of the N. nave arcade remains as an elongated bracket respond with nail head, recalling the plainer ones at Hartburn and hinting at superior quality in the work which is lost. There was also an aisle or transept on the S. side, where an original lancet remains in the E. wall. This transept is now a memorial chapel with appropriate and typical coloured glass by L. C. Evetts.

RYAL. All Saints.

The modest rebuilt chapel stands where lanes cross at the high windswept hamlet, whose western fringe commands a distant view reaching to far crags of the Roman Wall. A visit in passing stirs the mind, for here within are Norman responds to the chancel arch with scalloped capitals, though perhaps rather 'made up'. Even more surprising is the remarkable collection of grave covers in the W. gable, which leaves us wondering how so many dwellers hereabouts could afford these memorials of the 12C and 13C, a topic to interest the local historian.

SEATON DELAVAL. Our Lady.

On the edge of the hall park and concealed from the busy adjoining road, Seaton Delaval is one of Northumberland's delightful architectural surprises. This is not apparent from the exterior, where the high nave walls and long straight chancel do not seem to fit any established pattern. Interest is quickened by the presence of a blocked slit window in the N. nave wall, its closest analogues probably being the 12C lights in this position at Old Bewick and Rock. Then we find the 14C tracery head of a three light window over the outer W. door, looking odd in what appears to be a modern porch, the explanation being that it was formerly the E. chancel window inserted here when replaced by a modern replica. It is one of the larger and more elaborate examples of tracery carved in a single stone in the often preferred local manner.

The view of the interior when we open the inner W. door is unforgettable (*plate 8*). Facing us are two Norman arches, part moulded and part with zigzag and billet ornament, resting upon extremely heavy and plain cushion capitals. This is the Norman plan of nave, choir and sanctuary, though the square end is unusual when there are twin arches and may point to remodelling. Then there are monuments to examine, notably a knight and lady of the 14C on either side of the chancel. These have much clear detail, such as the jewelled collar to the lady's mantle, and it looks as if they may have been joined together on a table tomb. It has already been plausibly suggested that the stone shields mounted over the W. door may have belonged to this; amongst them we find the shield of the Delaval family, ermine two bars vert. On the nave walls is a majestic series of hatchments, now beautifully restored; all of which calls for some quiet moments of contemplation.

In leaving, notice the weathered carved tympanum over the inner W. door, easily missed by eyes not yet adjusted to the dim light, or overcome by the sight of the interior.

SHILBOTTLE. St. James.

Church looks, and is, of substantially modern build. Yet it incorporates interesting fossil remnants of an early 12C building, comprising a S. door with arch resting on colonnettes, one or two narrow slit windows and especially, the former chancel arch of two square orders and a chamfered hood, now re-used as an arch to the N. transept. The work is plain, with an affinity to that found at Thockrington. As at that church, there was no medieval development of the plan, but there was a continuing medieval presence, illustrated by the small tower house now embedded in the nearby vicarage, and emphasised by modern battlements and turret.

SIMONBURN. St. Mungo.

Church is pleasantly situated at the end of the village, a more imposing building than its surroundings would seen to warrant. Its appearance is that of a large 13C church with only a bell turret, closely resembling Haltwhistle. However, we do not see it today quite as the 13C builders left it, for Simonburn has been drastically rebuilt, albeit with much of the original material and largely to the original plans.

Inside, there is a notable feeling of spaciousness, coupled with a distinct downward slope of the floor towards the east. The aspect of the nave is characteristically severe, but in the chancel there are pleasing touches. First among these is the double piscina with a credence shelf above in a recess with matching moulded surround. This suggests a date at the turn of the 13C and 14C, the double bowl being found also at St. Andrew's in Newcastle. The Simonburn chancel then belongs to the time when the lancet style was giving way to developments in which large tracery windows were to be a dominant feature. This can be seen most clearly if we look at the western end of the chancel exterior, and make the reasonable assumption that what we see reproduces the original design. For next to the priest's door with its deep rich mouldings is a low side window of two lights with its head pierced by a simple pointed oval or vesica shape, the most elementary form of tracery. So we can visualise the natural successor to the Simonburn chancel being that of Newbiggin with its bar tracery windows.

This church represents Northumbrian 13C at its most developed, but that the site was in use much earlier is implied by the fragment of pre-Conquest cross shaft in the porch, with its vine stem pattern in flowing curves.

STAMFORDHAM. St. Mary.

The best way to approach Stamfordham church is from the west, by the road which leads from Fenwick, for then one sees it across the meadows, its tower close to the edge of an abrupt knoll overlooking the low former fen land (*plate 2*). One sees, too, how the ridge of the nave roof is set high on the tower, and comes down nearly in one sweep of steep pitch to the low aisle eaves. So to a considerable extent we can recapture the look of a typical 13C church, except that the imagination has somehow to bypass the aggressively red colour of the current covering.

The lancet and belfry lights of the tower would suit a date around 1200. The latter have twin pointed openings separated by a slender shaft with capital and base, and edged with a bold roll moulding, yet with only a plain tympanum over. The addition of a broad stepped buttress on the W. points to the risk of settlement from the sudden drop in ground level.

Stamfordham church is one of those where we feel regret at the thoroughness of Victorian rebuilding, the nave by Benjamin Ferrey scholarly but cold, the foliage capitals stiff and formal. In original medieval work, one often finds that capitals and bases, for instance, vary slightly in size, and though all may bear a similar sequence of mouldings or chamfers, the individual members are not absolutely identical. So the appearance is softened by the hand of the craftsman, whereas Victorian capitals have an exact machine precision introducing an impersonal element which is less in keeping. At any rate, those disposed to ponder the issue might find a useful starting point at Stamfordham.

The chancel, restored by John Dobson, does still disclose something of the fine lancet layout, and there is some original detail such as the most delicate dogtooth ornament round the rim of the tomb recess on the N. side. This houses, rather awkwardly, the figure of a priest in mass vestments. In a plainer recess on the S. side is a knight bearing a shield with the Fenwick arms. And on the chancel floor is the upper part of another knight elaborately carved in an apparent sandstone imitation of alabaster sculpture. The profuse fine detail such as the feather plume on his helmet is worth close inspection. A similar intention appears in the figures at the side of the Grey tomb at Chillingham. A quite different type of carving is to be seen in the fragment of altar back built into the E. end of the S. aisle, where the grimness of the crucifixion scene is augmented by the grotesquely crude yet compelling carving, by someone who did not allow lack of technique to hinder the transmission of his message. The group of fittings indeed give an insight into the medieval scene which would alone justify a visit to Stamfordham.

STANNINGTON. St. Mary.

Has a very fine Victorian west tower by R. J. Johnson forming a prominent landmark; something which late medieval Northumberland could neither have afforded nor desired. But of the interesting late 12C church which once stood on the site there remains only a hint in the respond capitals of the N. arcade with water leaf carving, and a fading photograph on the wall. Two of the three fragments of coloured glass in the vestry window are medieval, one being a 14C shield with the blazon gules three crowns or, as adopted by Tynemouth Priory.

THOCKRINGTON.
St. Aidan.

The small Norman church stands prominently on high ground some seven miles west of Belsay, seemingly afloat among rolling green hillocks with even today, remarkably few buildings in sight (*plate 7*). Although of modest size, it can be seen from a surprising distance, such as the road which climbs from Sweethope Lough towards Ridsdale.

Externally there is at first sight little sign of antiquity, for much of the nave is rebuilt and most windows are recent. That is, until we notice a round headed slit window in the chancel and a taller lancet in its E. wall. Expectations are amply fulfilled when we enter, for there are two plain 12C arches defining the choir space, with a round tunnel vault between. It is not certain whether there was a sanctuary beyond, for the ground falls away steeply close to the E. end. This simple and lonely church has known prominent people in its congregation, for the W. end is a handsome grave cover with a sword and beside it a worn but strangely appealing lady's effigy.

The rugged bell turret is likely to be a replacement for an earlier one, and the deep stepped buttress which supports it suggests misgivings about the stability of the W. gable, such as there probably had been about the E. Yet it is entirely in keeping with the type of building and the open landscape setting, which combine to offer a resort of memorable peace.

WARDEN. St. Michael and All Angels.

Warden church enjoys a remarkably secluded position near the junction of the north and south Tyne and the churchyard, especially when blowing with daffodils, provides a fine rural setting. It belongs to the group in which a 13C transeptal church retains an earlier tower. Lack of convincing detail has led to conflicting opinions about the date of this tower, but the slit windows with sloping or monolithic jambs, large quoins and crude tower arch suggest a pre-Conquest manner perhaps showing the influence of Bywell and Ovingham.

The nave and chancel have been extensively rebuilt in the 18C and 19C but they maintain the original plan and there is genuine 13C work in the aisleless transepts. The original windows are all of lancet form, the N. transept including two set close together and combined under one arch internally. This was a first stage in the evolution of the tracery window, as noted in the description of Heddon above, though the builders would surely have been surprised at the forms, which developed from their innovation.

For the rest we may perhaps be struck by the way in which the ends of these long unaisled transepts are remote from the body of the church, and wonder what particular purpose they were intended to serve.

A medieval monument in the chancel calls for notice, the remarkably complete grave cover in the form of a roof covered with tiles, a 'domus ultima'. Complete examples are rare, to be found in Hexham Abbey and the post-medieval old church of Whitfield; there are fragments in the porches of Bolam and Simonburn.

WARKWORTH. St. Lawrence.

Warkworth church is best approached from the north, when we see a Norman exterior rivalled only by the chancel of Norham. The very long nave is almost complete, with gabled N. door and row of round-headed windows (*plate 10*). Large buttresses were added in the 19C to counteract an ominous outward lean, partly caused by a 15C clerestory, which was then removed. The relative narrowness of the nave can be seen by moving round the W. end, the aisle wall being built against it leaving a vertical straight joint in the masonry. The tower, of later 12C build, has had a short medieval spire added, one of two surviving in the county, the other being at Newbiggin. The windows of the wide S. aisle are much restored, but the porch by which we enter is of sumptuous build, with a rib vaulted basement and a room above, the only example of its kind in the county (*plate 42*).

A first view of the interior gives the feeling of a double nave, so great is the width of the S. aisle. Yet we can, from a suitable viewpoint, still sense how the length, and dimness, of the Norman nave lead us on to the chancel, which has a rib vault in two bays, a rare concept forming a fitting adjunct, the ribs bearing horizontal zigzag after the pattern of Durham cathedral vaults. The chancel arch has uncommon decoration comprising a shallow shell shaped motif distinct from the deeply cut forms more usual in Norman ornament. An addition on the N. side is assumed to be a vestry and has a slotted opening in its W. wall.

The S. aisle is separated from the nave by an arcade of five bays of refined design with high bases, moulded arches, and capitals of basically 14C pattern. It stands apart from the often rudimentary construction of provincial builders of northern England at that time, and betokens skills not usually available except by wealthy patronage. A hint of its former aspect is afforded by the fragments of 15C glass collected in the tracery lights of the E. window. This has been made up with pieces of brightly coloured recent glass, but examination will soon disclose the muted shades of original pieces, which include figures labelled Scta Hilde and Meldreda.

At the W. end of the aisle is a well preserved effigy of a 14C knight with calm and striking features and showing below the surcoat a rare form of armour made up from scales rather like a tiled roof. The shield is quite distinct but he has not been certainly identified and the inscription on the ill-matched tomb cannot refer to this knight. Of more recent furnishings, the attractive iron communion rails, of early 18C date, are specially worthy of notice.

Warkworth is an imposing church, which seems never to have lacked funds for building and maintenance. The fact that it was bestowed by Henry I with other rich benefices on his chaplain might account for the original ambitious plan, just as in the early 14C Richard of Potesgrave, chaplain to Edwards II and III, was able to fund the splendid chancel of Heckington in Lincolnshire. And so long as the castle remained a residence of the Percies, we could expect this status to be preserved.

WHALTON. St. Mary Magdalene.

The exterior of this church does not at once reveal its medieval delights and one is aware of mainly Victorian windows, albeit of good design. The tower is original, with marks of two successive roofs on its E. face. It is difficult to date since architectural detail is lacking, but is probably 12C very, much repaired due to repeated settlement.

On a first visit, one is unprepared to find on entering an almost perfect 13C interior comprising nave with aisles to N. and S. and chancel with a N. aisle (*plate 21*). The nave arcades of three bays have octagonal columns and bases, with capitals of the 'long' type, and on the S. the hood mouldings have carved head stops (*plate 23*), one of them possibly commemorating an important donor. Several chamfer stops are carved in the form of a leaf. In the S. aisle wall are two pointed recesses, evidently rear arches of former lancet windows, for their sills may be detected outside. These show how low the original aisle walls would be, as may also be seen by continuing the sloping roof lines on the tower wall, and it is not difficult to understand why they were heightened to allow larger windows. The E. window of the aisle is a double light with simple tracery, and the adjoining piscina indicates the presence of a side altar, as frequently found in this position. Nearby on the S. wall is a fragment of pattern painting. All this supersedes a Norman nave which has yet left the imprint of its dimensions and a more definite trace in the squat round W. respond of the N. aisle with its heavy square capital.

The chancel too, was rebuilt in the 13C, though much of its upper walling is post-medieval, and it has the wide high arch on relatively low supports which is a recurring element in local design. There was a contemporary N. aisle later widened to form a chapel, and two arches rest at their centre on a remarkable column which confers a unique distinction on the church (*plate 20*). It is square in plan with shafts at each corner, and between them are vertical strips of very large dogtooth ornament. The whole unit seems intended for a more spacious environment, and might draw upon patterns used in one of the greater churches, as in the presbytery of Tynemouth priory.

Of later furnishing, there is a well-preserved Georgian Royal Arms of the kind used from 1801 to 1814, and a chancel screen of the 1890s by Ralph Hedley, with a later rood group of 1915. Notice the subtle inclusion in the screen carving of a motif based on the fragment of wall painting in the S. aisle.

WHITTINGHAM. St. Bartholomew.

Has a commanding position on a low knoll at the west end of the village, and is a transeptal church of considerable size with W. tower, and features for a visitor which are both fascinating and tantalising. For here was undoubtedly a pre-Conquest church of prominent status, of which the lower part of the tower and its arch with repaired crown remain. The upper part of the tower was demolished and rebuilt in the 1840s in a way which today would be regarded as irresponsible. The remaining part is of two dates, for at a height of about six feet the style of the corner stones changes from bulky pieces set alternately to a sequence which to the eye recalls the pillar and clasping stones designated 'long and short' in more finished southerly examples. It is satisfying to see that a similar structural change occurs in the W. gable of the nave, which may be traced by vertical straight joints in the masonry on each side of the tower. Traces of the E. corners also remain so that we know the long narrow dimensions of the early nave, though all that we can see of its walls is a teasingly incomplete beginning of an arch at the NW corner inside. Whether the entrance to a chapel or the beginning of an arcade, is perhaps a point for the visitor to ponder. One detail which should not be missed is the miniscule pellet ornament at the springing of the tall tower arch.

The jambs of the chancel arch resemble those of Alnham church, suggesting that the chancel had been renewed by about 1200, and a reminder that surviving architecture of this period tends to cluster in the Aln valley at Alnham, Whittingham, Lesbury and the lost old church of Alnmouth. The present chancel is 18C with 19C windows.

Then we turn to the S. arcade, essentially a 13C design though evidently, from the date 1697 carved upon its W. pillar, a partial rebuild of the 17C. It has a distinctive decoration of chamfer stops carved with one and a half units of dogtooth, an unusual treatment which, as noted many years ago, recurs in the arcades of Embleton church, which appear to be by the same mason. We may add to this the remark that the foliaged brackets from which the arcade springs are also of similar design at the two churches, as are some circular medallion hood stops.

Next there is a phase of about 1300, represented by two three-light windows, one looking into the vestry, the other in the N. aisle. Both have bar tracery, in each instance carved from a single stone. This technique may be widespread where suitable stone is available and Northumberland has more then 30 examples, some of large size. Neither window is necessarily in its original position, but they indicate a considerable building effort about the time that the new chancel of Newbiggin was being built in a similar style, schemes whose spread was to be inhibited by the poverty of a war stricken 14C.

The remaining history of Whittingham is a sad one of neglect followed by regrettable rebuilding. As well as the upper tower, an interesting N. arcade of round, possibly Norman arches was removed and replaced by a free copy of the S. arcade. The balance was partly redressed when the tower arch was repaired and exposed to view and an original piscina opened up in the S. transept; the rib-vaulted porch in the style of Ponteland has possibly been renewed. The sight of hatchments on the nave walls is particularly welcome, fragile and vulnerable as these memorials are.

WIDDRINGTON. Holy Trinity.

Widdrington church can easily be missed by those who hurry along the busy coastal route to Amble and Warkworth, for it stands well above the road, screened by sheltering trees. And to miss Widdrington is to forego an unexpected and warming experience of medieval architecture (*plate 32*).

From the outside, interest is awakened when one sees the windows, square headed with simple 14C tracery, sometimes carved in a single stone

The chancel is longer than the short nave, which has its S. door set very close to the W. gable. That S. door has an arch decked with the shadows of deep rich mouldings, closely similar to the transept arch at Woodhorn.

Facing us within is the N. aisle arcade, with concave bell capitals and square abacus telling of the late 12C, though the aisle wall is modern and in fact these arches were at one time blocked with masonry. Then, looking towards the chancel and the S. aisle, there is a complete picture of rural 14C architecture (*plate 33*). Perhaps because of the shortness of the nave, the aisle is extended along the S. wall of the chancel to form a chapel, with piscina showing the site of a side altar. So it comes about, that the wide chancel arch is supported by the E. pillar of the S. arcade, and as the thrust is imperfectly balanced, this column has canted over to the S. to an extent clearly visible to the eye. Four arches thus bear on one column, a daring piece of construction which was nearly disastrous, but which gives a charmingly open aspect to this part of the church.

The chancel E. window though small, has flowing tracery of the 14C featuring horizontal flame-like elements, uncommon in the district; there is an example in the N. transept of Durham cathedral. In the N. wall are two recesses evidently to house tombs, with moulded hoods. The one to the E. is higher and has a stone shield bearing the arms of Widdrington, the notable local family whose castle and mansion, now vanished, immediately adjoined the church to the east. This position in the chancel is often chosen for the burial of a leading patron, and it is plausible to suppose that the 14C reconstruction of Holy Trinity was largely funded by the Widdringtons, being beyond the means of the thinly populated chapelry of Newbiggin. But notice that the plain sedilia are economically formed by a lowered sill to the S. chancel window, as at Heddon and Newbiggin, though there is a second piscina oddly placed at the E. end of the seat.

This delightful interior has a most welcoming appearance and is beautifully kept. Perhaps it is seen at its best on an autumn or winter day when a brilliant low sun strikes through the windows and casts their form on the flags, rendering the whole scene luminous.

WOODHORN. St. Mary.

The nave of Woodhorn church is now a museum where interesting exhibitions of crafts and other themes are mounted by the local authority. An unexpected result is that the varied architectural features of the interior can be seen much more easily than when it was part of a church. And they show an extended progression of styles. The core of the nave is often accepted as Anglo-Saxon, and it is evident that the high windows are earlier than the Norman arches of the arcades, which cut through their lower parts. The columns on the N. side are thick and squat, the scalloped capitals heavy and square, as in the remaining aisle column at Whalton. The S. arcade provides a contrast, for there we can see how the round arched system of building was being refined and that builders had learned by experience that more slender columns would bear a high compressive, that is vertical, loading. Also that capitals could be made both visually and actually lighter by giving a concave instead of a convex outline. Nailhead round the bases adds a decorative touch as in the arcade of similar date at Edlingham.

These arcades are extended by wide transept arches, that on the N. with rich deep mouldings consistent with a mid 13C date. This arch springs from a bracket with delicate foliage carving, with which the large head beneath looks a little out of keeping.

The chancel is essentially Victorian though preserving the appearance of lancet windows. It contains on the N. side a lady's effigy with delightful though damaged miniature figures at the feet and drawing the headdress away from her features. Authorities have noted other hints of a religious connection, but her precise status remains uncertain.

Of medieval building there remains to note only the lower part of the tower, sturdy and Norman looking with a curious low relief statue built into the W. face. Fragmentary remains are numerous and usefully annotated comprising carved Anglo Saxon pieces and a group of later medieval grave covers two of which bear the strange emblem light heartedly known as a hockey stick but more seriously interpreted as a builder's instrument or pilgrim's staff.

REFLECTIONS.

BYWELL ON TYNE

Here where the curve of murmuring river
Borders a space of hallowed ground
Where in the prime of summer falls cool shade
From stately trees that fringe St. Peter's round
There long lancets now proclaim the art
Achieved by master mason of renown
And strange high windows of the nave
Bespeak the mystery of dream-like past.
A short field's length away St. Andrew's tower
Aspires to greet the morning sun, as it has done
Since Anglo Saxon thegn knew this as home;
Now wearing benediction of the years
In furrows of red stone, a sight to call back time
And yield a feeling of mature wine.

Twin churches set by level lawns, with river
Mirroring an ever changing sky,
While turrets of the castle tint anew
With romance, such a scene as Bewick drew.

KIRKHARLE

As reeds on Severnside that Elgar knew,
Long grasses whisper in this churchyard too
Slanting towards the silvered east whence rise,
Pearled shining clouds of April's blue grey skies
To frame a bright fanfare of daffodil.
Or, mark the ease of seamless summer days
When silently we sit and seem to gaze
Through mists of time down centuries to meet
A master mason's eyes and hear him say
"So build, that what you leave may outlast time"
And his men in their turn hold fast his dream
Bequeathing us those living shapes in stone
That now sleep gently midst the rustling view
Searched out by sun and shadow, holding for ever new
Those truths which stirred their hands of old
Embodied here that all may see, while far around
The breezes sift and sift, to move us with their sound.

NEWBIGGIN BY THE SEA

*Softly the swell surges about the point
As the shadows pass, and the sunlight fades and glows
On age old fretted stones that the winds have known.
Within all is light and the whispering sound of the waves,
And a sense of the worship of ages that seems to anoint
And blend with the crispness of moulding and stone.
The march of striding arches leads the eye
To the east where a rainbow vision of holiness glows,
And brightness steals along the pillars printing upon the flags
The curving tracery forms of smiling window heads
Till at noon the sunbeam touches a flowered cross,
A gentle pattern of faith that knows no fear.
The day wears on, the light fades softly,
As flames of candles point the mellowing shades
While deeper sounds the wash of the waves.
Soon night will enfold this place of peace
And the bow of the moon shed a dreamlight on the bay
Long ages have left their mark and have passed away,
Yet ever upon the sounding point will be
The living house of prayer and the surge of the sea.*

OLD BEWICK.

Here in a secret hollow known to the ageless hills,
Where the rich cream flowered shrub
Is drowsy with the praise of myriad bees
Find then the presence of the Lord
In far antiquity of slotted stone
And see how double arches finely wrought
Are heralds to the rounded altar throne.
Here is a peace that searches inner thought
To bid us pause amidst the stir
Of restless hasting world; yet mindful of its snares
Stare cat-like features whence the arches spring.
But see the quiet sunlight gently touch
These roughened stones that link us with the past
And hear, as first stars of the evening come,
How slowly then the dell will fill
With restful creed of glittering rill
That threads the churchyard edge.

THOCKRINGTON.

We leave the gold-green tinted lanes
To find the church beneath an open sky,
Seen from afar, outstanding on its knoll
Riding green upland waves as if a ship
Moving with grey clouds racing from the west.
A high wind calling from the turret's rugged form
Hisses in churchyard grass as if the spray were flying
While autumn's crisp and piercing light reveals
Each facet of a weathered stone and sets
The whole church shining; here within,
The tumult of the outer world is muted
Soft as the glancing light that swells and dies
Along the walls and through the arch
To rest on cross and frontal and proclaim
We too are moving forward on a journey
Charged with a hope that says – all shall be well.

See the carved floral cross so aptly wrought,
Nearby the worn effigy in stone that countless years
The weather played upon, yet still to inward eye appear
The folds of dress, the features calm; all touched
With visions fragile as the shadow of a lark.

Look forth again and note how yet afar
The pearl grey veil of coming shower
Steals from the view the fading distant crags
While scattered sheep like boulders lined with fleece
Are gathering to drift down wind worn ways.

Night falls, the air grows still,
Last afterglow has faded yet there lingers
In the west a luminous blue as deep
As peacock's plumage, hung with diamonds.
And dark against its gleam the outline of the church
A vessel now becalmed and deep at rest,
Full laden with the burden of the past.

WHALTON

High summer and the winding lane
Is fringed with meadow sweet,
While over all the buoyant clouds
Drift poised on scented heat.
We thrust along the dusty way to find
Cool shade within the churchyard gate
And cooler still the peaceful nave,
Silent and dim yet quick
With that soft essence which declares
The presence of old lamps.
Four-petalled flowers deck the sides
Of that fair column which divides
The chancel from its aisle;
And did the sculptor think of One
Who felt the suns of Galilee and loved
The flowers of its fields?
Scarce breathing we ascend the tower stairs
To gaze into the stillness of the nave.
Here no movement marks the way of time,
Save the slow turning shafts of sun
That pool the flags and finger honeyed stone
While yet without, the pageant of the day
Fades slowly from the glow of shining noon.
Resting we pause, to carry through long years
The calming presence sensed within this hour,
While steadily the gold grows in the west
And those warm homeward lanes
Are drowsy with the song of summer.

WIDDRINGTON

Wool clouds streaming down the bright spring skies,
Flying shadows skimming with the breeze,
By the Easter garden the light will flare and pass
To touch a shining pew, and carved stone shield
Emblazoned where a founder's memory dwells.

The slowly moving pageant of the year
Brings once again long sunlit days of summer.
The Cheviots loom softly through the haze,
As brooding clouds are gathering over the plain
And steadily the heat mounts with the day.
Inside the church cool peace and silence reign
While gently through the open door there breathes
An essence of the noon-still scent of roses.
With evening comes the distant wash of waves;
A whispered scurrying of small wild things
While in the azure haze there slowly grows
The pallid vellum outline of the moon.

Autumn skies of cobalt dazzle with low sun,
Slashed with russet gold above the shadows inky blue.
The hills are sharp and clear where on lonely walks of sheep,
The tingling breeze is laced with curlew's call.
Here in the sheltered chapel, stones shine honey-warm,
Roses flashing gold and crimson deck the umber shade
Long shapes of windows on the floor are thrown,
As though some artist's brush full charged
With glowing sunlight swept across the flags.

Then see, the ground now hard with grey frost rime,
Within the church chill silence sharp with echoes.
Yet soon a host of candles gleam on eager children's faces
As slowly dimming arches merge into the shade
And we are part of history begun,

When first those arches from their pillars sprung.
The windows shine within a dark outline
Against an afterglow of fading rose and gold
The sunken way is brimmed with pearly mist while high above,
Bright stars in sable velvet shape the Plough.

As grip of winter lessens, soon again there will be seen
The crystal glint of snowdrops that by the altar stand.
The wayward breeze will ring again the bells of daffodil
And champagne days of spring be close at hand.

———————————————————